"Retirement, a Dream . . .
Your Journey, the Challenge"

Grandpa's
Rocking Chair

Vern Schultz

authorHOUSE®

AuthorHouse™
1663 Liberty Drive
Bloomington, IN 47403
www.authorhouse.com
Phone: 1 (800) 839-8640

Published by AuthorHouse 03/13/2018

ISBN: 978-1-5462-3244-5 (sc)
ISBN: 978-1-5462-3243-8 (e)

Library of Congress Control Number: 2018902935

Print information available on the last page.

This book is printed on acid-free paper.

Contents

Contents

Preface

Age has a funny way of creeping up on you. One day you wake up and to your surprise eighty-eight years have crept by without any warning. It's hard to believe I've lived five years longer than my dad who died at eighty-three, and I considered him really old—almost an antique! As a youngster, I thought I'd have my youth forever, and it was just those old people like my parents and grandparents that got old but certainly not me. But reality has set in, and the curse of old age is staring me in the face and in my bones. I am pleased that my heart is still pumping, my legs and arms still work, and my inner vessels are patched up with that amazing wire mesh and new 3M glue. Just don't ask me to run or walk too far, to hear what you said without my hearing aid, and, oh yes, don't ask what happened yesterday. On the positive side, however, I'm still capable of driving, can see quite well to read, and eating is still one of my favorite pleasures. All in all I am able to mingle in society without being viewed as different. Old, yes, but not different.

What do we old people do when turning ninety is just around the corner? Well, in my case I gave up jogging but still take walks when the urge hits me. I enjoy walking with a cane even though I don't need it yet! It gives me that distinguished look, sort of a feeling of importance. Another positive attribute that piggy backs with old age is the increased time us old fogies have for "thinking," to sit in our rocking chairs and remember back to those positive times in our life, those events we wish we could change, those things we could or should have done, and activities we would still like to do if only we were twenty years younger. I think we also become more philosophical in our senior years. I've asked myself many times over what influenced me in my life's decision making. Why did I function so conservatively compared to others? Why was I so hesitant to take more chances? What motivated me to work multiple jobs. Why was I described as "cheap" in financial matters? And why didn't I expose myself to the more exciting and fun social mores of the day? But the million-dollar question that I ponder most often is, "How in the world did I go from 'zero' financial resources at age twenty-two to living in an upscale all-inclusive retirement living Center with money to spare at age eighty-eight?" I never was in the six-figure income bracket, and my wife was a stay-at-home mom and didn't work till way later in our marriage, so just what amazing event led me from being Mr. Conservative to living this wonderful carefree retirement life?

The answer to this million-dollar question became very clear to me one day as I sat comfortably in my rocking chair in the front veranda of my retirement home. I realized that unknowingly I was following the same lifestyle, the same conservative living pattern that my parents followed throughout their lives that led them to their comfortable retirement life residing in the Texas valley. Apparently, they had educated me well. It took all of these years to realize I had registered and passed the Art Schultz Economics 101 course that if listed in a college syllabus would most likely be titled, A Guide to Conservative Living. This course was based on the techniques my dad used to survive the Great Depression. As you may have guessed, Art Schultz is my dad. As a teenager I figured my parents, especially my dad, were really square, out of sync with the times, and, to be perfectly honest, I considered them tight as a drum, as did many of their relatives. It took me till my midthirties to realize that maybe they weren't so out of it as I thought, and when I reached forty I realized, by golly, they really did know what they were talking about and were with the times 100 percent. Now at eighty-eight years old, I realize how wise they were and that it was their influence, their example, that played a significant role in determining the lifestyle I was to follow. My parents are no longer with us, but I'm sure they would be pleased to learn, and most likely surprised, that I did pass the mythical Art Schultz Economics 101 course with flying colors. This course has made it possible for their son to fully enjoy sitting comfortably in his retirement rocking chair today. How wrong I was to label my folks tight. They were frugal, another word for smart. I guess that also makes me frugal… but smart, I'm not sure! I wonder if my kids consider me tight or frugal. I don't plan to ask!

This book was written for the purpose of sharing the content of the mythical Art Schultz Economics 101 course with all those folks who are trying to survive this challenging world we are living in today. The book is directed primarily at that growing population of young folks who find themselves operating in the low to medium income group, struggling to survive and stay out of debt, and who truly want to enjoy some semblance of the good life. A comfortable retirement in later life may still be just a distant dream. Some older folks may also enjoy this book allowing them to compare their lifestyle over the past eighty-plus years with mine. My feelings won't be hurt to have a few old-timers disagree with my observations. Thirty-seven years of officiating football and basketball have left me with thick skin. This Art Schultz Economics 101 is not a formal course with a syllabus to follow. It really is a suggested lifestyle that if followed should help attain the financial resources necessary for an enjoyable standard of living and hopefully fulfill that retirement dream. This lifestyle plan, based on surviving the Great Depression, worked for my folks, it worked for my wife and me, and I bet it will work for you as well. Be aware that it may require some changes in your living habits and, yes, even some sacrifices. Remember this saying: "If it's easy anyone can do it; if it's hard only a few will try!"

SECTION 1

Living Frugal to Survive

CHAPTER 1

Looking Back

I remember, like it was yesterday, that final visit I had with my mother before she passed away. She was residing in the North Ridge Nursing Home and closing in on her one-hundredth birthday. She was looking forward to reaching that magic one-hundred-year-old milestone, and receiving the congratulatory letter from the president. My mother's mind was sharp as a tack at her advanced age, and we had an absolutely wonderful visit that afternoon talking about the family, her past life, and the fact that she was the last of her generation to survive. During our visit my mom said something that really got me thinking. She said, "Your dad and I began our married life with nothing and made it through that awful Depression, and over the years we accumulated everything we needed. We had it all. Later in life we had just a wonderful retirement that included traveling, living those warm winters in the Texas valley, and enjoying the fruits of our labor. Now I'm back at the beginning again, with nothing … just that dresser against the wall that your dad and I bought the year we were married." In that simple statement, she described to me "the circle of life," something all of us must face in time. She went on to explain that those last thirty years in retirement were the most enjoyable years of her life and hoped that I would enjoy my retirement years just as much. Unfortunately, my mother passed away just shy of her one-hundredth birthday, a week after our visit, so she never received that president's congratulatory letter. I'll always remember my mother's comments at that final visit.

It's true that we all will face this "circle of life" my mother described to me, if we are fortunate to live those extended years like my mom. The $10,000 question to be asked is, "Will you be able to live that great life, similar to my mom's, as part of your "circle of life"? I was fortunate to successfully make it through my forty-plus-year working career and these past twenty-five years of retirement by carefully following the Art Schultz Economic 101 course, Guide to Conservative Living, with a few adaptations added. I suggest you consider registering for this course as well.

My primary concern back in the early 1950s as a twenty-two-year-old rookie worker, was making enough money to keep food on the table and my beautiful wife happy ... probably your feelings as well. Retirement at that time was simply a distant dream, but as my mother pointed out, it is an important part of one's "Circle of Life." As years passed I came to the realization that a successful retirement required adequate money in the savings account. As my grandmother said so often, "You can't live on pants buttons." Retiring with an empty savings account could end up being a nightmare rather than an enjoyable dream. This book is all about building a financial plan of action early in your work career allowing you to live "the good life," leading in time to a comfortable and enjoyable retirement. My dad's mythical Economics 101 course, based on a conservative and practical approach to financial planning, was the guide I followed throughout my work career and led me to this comfortable rocking chair. Who knows, if you follow the suggested guidelines described in this book you just might end up taking over my rocking chair! Before reading any further, let me whet your appetite a bit and give you a taste of what an enjoyable retirement day can offer. Just remember, retirement is the end, not the beginning. The beginning is your real challenge!

This past Monday my wife and I had just finished lunch with good friends in our retirement residence restaurant. The meal was over, but the conversation never stopped. Those hour-and-a-half lunches were becoming routine, only to cease when they shut the lights off hoping we would take the hint. How different from my old working days when a twenty- or thirty-minute lunch break was a luxury. Later that afternoon a country music group was on our entertainment schedule to be followed by a leisurely dinner that might take up a two-hour time slot. After dinner, a few of us residents who are sports fans headed to the Rathskeller room to watch the football game on one TV and the baseball game on the other TV, with Coke and popcorn on the house. It was a busy and exhausting day. You know, living in a retirement residence is just like belonging to a fancy country club! It sounds pretty inviting, doesn't it?

I must admit this carefree life is much more enjoyable then those many stress-filled days during my working career. It also takes precedent over those never-ending chores I'd be doing if my wife and I had decided to stay in the home we had lived in for the past twenty-four years. We built this home from scratch and loved that country living, but maintaining this home in tip-top shape was starting to wear on us. Just walking down to the pole barn was beginning to test my lung capacity. Today, for example, I would most likely have had the choice of cutting and trimming the grass, repairing a fence, feeding horses, or cutting back those shrubs that seemed to grow a foot each day. This move to our retirement residence offers a whole new leisurely lifestyle that is right up my alley. I enjoyed all those yard and home building tasks till I reached eighty-five, and then, to be perfectly honest, they lost their luster. I'm convinced this move will add to my longevity and is a pretty positive sign that the dreaded Alzheimer's curse hasn't hooked me yet. Now if only I could remember where I put my car keys!

A favorite pastime, when not involved in one of the residence's many activities, is relaxing in my favorite rocking chair out in the front porch area. There's always the chance for some good conversation, with the weather being one of the most common topics of each day. A number of the residents came from farm families, and some still own their farm and rent out the land, so I've learned quite a bit about farm living. As a child, I never had the opportunity to visit a farm, so by keeping my mouth shut and just listening to some great farm stories, it's been quite a learning experience. For example, the other day one of the residents sitting in the rocking chair next to me commented on how beautiful this day was, and then asked if I had noticed the house just two blocks east on Main Street that was built from a Sears and Roebuck catalog plan design. He said this house was constructed some sixty years ago with all materials purchased from the Sears and Roebuck catalog. I told him that as kids we read that two-inch-thick catalog from cover to cover but never knew it included house plans and building materials. He said, "You may have spent time reading the catalog, but on our farm, we used it ... every page. It served as toilet paper in our outhouse." I asked if the Sears catalog didn't contain toilet paper for sale. He said, "Toilet paper cost money, and the Sears catalog was free." It got me thinking that living in the city maybe wasn't so bad after all. I'm not so sure outhouse facilities and milking those cows every morning and night was my thing anyway!

That rocking chair has proven to be one of my favorite spots to just sit back, share stories with my neighbors, and spend time reminiscing on my past life plus trying to predict what the future might look like, whether I'll be a part of it or not. At eighty-eight years of age, I realize there's not much I can do to change the past, and I'm not aware of any law against guessing what the future holds, but it keeps the mind active. My doctor tells me the secret to reaching ninety is to stay physically active and keep my mind busy. I do everything my doctor tells me (and my wife as well). It seemed like I seldom had the time or maybe just didn't take time, during my working years, to sit back, relax, and do any serious thinking. It seemed there was always something more important to do. Now I've got time on my hands to relax in my rocking chair and try to figure out if I made a difference in this world or if all I did was waste time, and to ponder what the future might hold ... if not for me, for my grandkids! I also have to admit that more than once I've sat in that chair and wondered, "How in the world did I survive all those challenging years and end up with enough money to live in such a nice place?"

My family was shocked when we shared the news with them that we were going to sell the homestead, move to a small town twenty miles away, and into a retirement residence. I honestly think they figured we were going to remain in the home we called Cedar Hills for the remainder of our lives ... and maybe even after that! You see, my two boys played a major role in the building of our home, and it was truly a family labor of love. My grandson hunted ducks, geese, and deer on our property, and each spring he would purchase fifteen to eighteen cattle to be fattened up in our fields for their sale in late fall. It also served as a site to get together as a family. So, you see, there was a personal touch that would be lost forever if we moved—kind of like a death in the family! After the shock regarding this move had worn off and our children and friends visited our new residence, it was apparent that their attitude had changed. They discovered that our apartment was quite spacious with two bedrooms, two baths, a den, and fireplace, plus all the amenities we had in our home. They enjoyed the restaurant, the Rathskeller party room, the heated garage, and the unique German architecture. I think what really impressed them was the realization that this setting offered an opportunity for their mom and me to enjoy a new life away from the responsibilities of work and those home/ farm activities that pretty well had us tied down ... and we were safe. I honestly believe certain family members viewed our new lifestyle as something they also hoped to experience when coming face-to-face with their retirement years. I remember my granddaughter sitting in the rocking chair next to me on the front porch saying, "Grandpa, I hope when I get old like you I'll be able to sit in your rocking chair."

"I said, 'I hope so too!'" Just another way of her saying, "I hope I can retire and live the good life that you're living here." When I responded with the comment, "I hope so too!" it was said with tongue in cheek, hoping it would really be true. You see, preparing for retirement in today's world is in no way comparable to the world I lived and worked in. The world my children and grandchildren are walking into is simply light years different from the working world I experienced. I retired twenty-five years ago, and in just this short period of time the economy, work climate, and living style have changed dramatically along with the rule book dealing with retirement. Many of the benefits I enjoyed during my work career are disappearing, and job security is simply up for grabs. There is little question that today's working world offers a greater challenge than in my time. Nothing would make me happier than to have my children and grandchildren take over my rocking chair. I plan to keep it warm for them. I wish them success!

It wouldn't surprise me if my grandchildren think that old grandpa, lounging comfortably in his rocking chair, lived the perfect life with few challenges or bumps in the road and that I never had a worry in the world. I never asked them and don't plan to, but as a youngster I also figured my grandparents traveled the easy road in life, that they just got old the easy way, surviving on grandma's great sugar cookies.

Later in life I learned the monumental challenges my grandparents and parents had to face just to survive those challenging Depression years of the 1930s. If you, the reader, believe you are the first generation facing a future that is loaded with economic obstacles and challenges standing in your way to success, put that dream to rest. Every generation since time began has been faced with challenges of one kind or other to survive ... only the challenges facing each generation are different. Here's hoping that makes you feel better. You are not alone!

Surviving the Great Depression of the 1930s was a major challenge for all of America. As bad and depressing as it was for our parents to make ends meet during those trying times, something good did occur. Our parents taught us children, by their example, how to live with few frills, get by with little money, and enjoy those simple things in life. They taught us a conservative approach to life that was embedded in our brains and still is fresh in our minds today. I adopted their conservative teachings in all facets of my life, and it has paid dividends for me. I take pride in being labeled conservative, some might say cheap, because this conservative lifestyle is the very reason I'm sitting in this retirement rocking chair today. To better understand my conservative personal and financial philosophy, allow me to share how living through that Great Depression, those terrible 1930s, influenced me from the very day I was born in 1929—the year of America's disastrous financial collapse. Let me share just a few experiences that come to mind, living in my hometown of Saint Paul, Minnesota, that typify the impact the Depression had on this community, the country in general, and, oh yes, on me!

CHAPTER 2

The Great Depression and Its Impact

Retirement was the very last thing in the minds of my parents and grandparents who found themselves right in the middle of the greatest depression of our country's history, which began in 1929 and extended right through the 1930s. To put it bluntly, our country at that time was at a financial standstill with little work and thousands of unemployed people. Retirement was absolutely the last thing on their minds. Survival was far more important! How in the world did those folks in that Great Depression of the 1930s survive when employment was at a standstill? It's interesting to study the various techniques our parents and grandparents used to get by on a little less than nothing and some of the unique approaches they used to save a buck in a nearly dead economy. Looking from another vantage point, it may give many young people entering the employment market today an appreciation of what folks had to face when employment was at a standstill, and of some of the unique solutions they came up with to survive in this trying period of American history. Who knows, maybe some of their survival tricks might still be useful today!

Let's recognize right off the bat that employment challenges are nothing new in America. If you plan well, and have the willingness to begin thinking out of the box for solutions, climbing the ladder to success is possible even in tough times. My parents were good at "climbing the ladder" that led to surviving those tumultuous years and, low and behold, led to their successful retirement in later years. I believe it's worth the time to look back to the 1930s and see how the folks in those days faced their everyday economic challenges and survived. Yes, it's true that our economic challenges today may not be the same as in my parents' day, but let's take a closer look at how they managed to survive and ended up "happy campers." It's an interesting story. One requirement in my high school English class was to read that famous book entitled *A Tale of Two Cities*. I remember the opening phrase of this book very well. "It was the best of times, it was the worst of times." As I look back on the Great Depression, I believe this same phrase would hold true. What a perfect way to describe this devastating period of American history; however, I promise never to use this phrase again to avoid being arrested for plagiarism or, worse yet, being harassed by all of America's English teachers.

America was on the rise right through the 1920s with business booming, the stock market making many folks rich, and America growing at an unprecedented rate. Then, without warning, the stock market crashed, the banks closed, and America came to an abrupt standstill. Panic occurred, particularly for those wealthy folks who overnight became dirt poor. There were an estimated twenty-seven thousand or more suicides a year in those early years of the Depression. Central Park in New York became known as "Shanty Town," with hundreds of shacks constructed to replace homes that were foreclosed. This pattern was occurring throughout the country, including our home state of Minnesota. Soup kitchens and bread lines to provide food for the new "poor" were set up, and hunger marches became common occurrences. It was a devastating period in America's history. It was the worst of times!

I just happened to enter this unsettled economic crisis in December of 1929. My dad told me I was probably the only positive event that occurred that year. Apparently, America's Great Depression that began in 1929 overshadowed my birth, which, at least for me, was a significant event. I'm not sure my folks even celebrated my arrival. I know they didn't celebrate the closing of all the banks, the massive unemployment taking place, folks jumping out of windows because of lost fortunes and utter confusion, and the absolute uncertainty of America's future. The attitude of folks during this depression apparently was like the feeling of despair some of us loyal Minnesota Twin fans get when the Twins go on a thirteen-game losing streak, and the New York Yankees arrive in town to begin a new series. In both instances these represent the "worst of times." Don't forget the "best of times" was my arrival on the scene! To survive in those troubled times required a positive approach to life (viewing the bottle as half full instead of half empty). Let's face the facts; it was a challenge trying to figure how to survive in the 1930s if you're out of work, your savings wiped out by the banking crisis, the pantry at home is empty, hardly any social agencies to offer support, and your grandparents are just as poor as you. In this environment, you're lucky to receive even a homemade holiday card for Christmas. If your family was hungry, some fathers in desperation turned to stealing food. If dad got caught and thrown in jail, he would most likely get food to eat, but his family would still go hungry, and that was the reason for stealing food in the first place. Not a very good solution! Oh, yes, I should mention that city soup kitchens were an alternative to starvation, but watered-down soup wasn't exactly one's favorite menu item!

We were one of the fortunate families. In those early 1930s, my dad had a job in a machine shop called Auto Engine Works, which was in St. Paul's Midway District, which was easy walking distance from our home, so no transportation expense. He did work six days a week and generally ten-hour days. His wages were minimal, but my memory tells me that we did have food on the table, indoor facilities, and the comforts of a coal-heated home. I have a vague memory of my dad and mother expressing concerns about the welfare of certain neighbors, a few friends, and even relatives who were out of work. I do recall one of my mother's relatives asking my dad for a loan. I know my dad reluctantly loaned him some money, and I think in time this loan was paid back, but I'm not sure. I discovered later in life that loaning money to family members might best be termed a gift!

In those frightening years with negative employment and progress at a standstill, how did those folks who were victims of these tough times survive? I enjoy watching the TV show *Shark Tank*, where folks present innovative ways of making money to this panel of financial millionaires in hopes one of them will finance their ideas, and they will soon become successful millionaires as well. That's exactly what those folks in the Great Depression wanted—to become successful but not necessarily millionaires. Unfortunately, they didn't have the *Shark Tank* to help them. They had to be clever and arrive at innovative ways on their own to survive. Let's look at just a few examples of how those folks in the 1930s tightened their belts to keep their head above water and not drown in depression. As my high school history teacher said that first day of class, "By studying history and the past, you can better avoid mistakes in planning for the future." Let's see if he was right!

Food on the Table

There was a knock on our front door in that stifling hot summer of 1934, and being a helpful four-year-old, I ran to the door and opened it. There stood a fellow I had never seen before. He said, "Hi, sonny, can I talk to your mother?" She followed me to the door and talked to him for a few minutes and then pointed to our garage. He tipped his cap to my mother, walked to the garage, took out the lawn mower, and began cutting the grass. I thought that was kind of funny because my dad had cut the grass just two days before. When he finished, my mother brought him a plate of hot food. He thanked her and proceeded to eat the food on our front stoop and then was on his way. I remember this very well even though it occurred many years ago, and I was still too young to attend school. It presented an interesting idea to me. I figured if I was hungry, all I had to do was knock on our neighbor Mrs. Pomplune's front door, ask to cut their grass, and be rewarded with a free meal. It was a bad idea because the lawn mower was too heavy for me to push anyway! Later that evening, my mother explained who that man was who knocked on the front door. She said he had offered to do some chores around the house if she would provide him with some food. He was hungry and had no money and could find no work. The Northern Pacific Railroad tracks were just a few blocks from our home, and he was riding trains from one town to another looking for work. She told me there was little work available, and thousands of men were seeking any job they could find. She also told me that this fellow wasn't a bum, an alcoholic, or a derelict looking for a free handout. He was labeled a "hobo." This was the term used to describe those men who rode the rails going from town to town desperately looking for work. By the way, these men rode on the outside of the train and slept in boxcars; they were not paying customers! These men were being very innovative in figuring out how to survive without money in their pockets and an absolute unknown future. This hobo, along with legions of others, had discovered a very cheap way to travel from town to town and avoid the expense of hotels, and had developed a unique approach to getting free food. They were living on the hope that tomorrow would be better than today and that a job and a new life was just waiting for them in the next town!

Fancy Eating Habits

There were no McDonald's or Burger King restaurants on every street corner in the 1930s as there are today. The only fast-food restaurant in those days was White Castle. Fortunately for me, one White Castle restaurant was located on the corner of Lexington and University in Saint Paul just three blocks from my home. You could order five of these hamburgers for a dime if you clipped a coupon out of the paper that made this great buy possible. Sitting at that counter with my dad sharing those five White Castle hamburgers was an absolute treat—a special occasion! Unfortunately, we didn't visit the White Castle restaurant often because securing that dime was a challenging task. Apparently, the dime in those days was probably equal to a dollar bill in today's economy, and my mom said that dime was needed for far more important items. At the time, I couldn't figure out what could possibly be more important than eating one of those delicious hamburgers.

Even though my dad had a job, we just never ventured out to eat in a "real" restaurant. My dad's attitude was, "Why waste hard-earned money on restaurant food when I need it more for work clothes, coal for the furnace, food on the table, or a baseball glove or an alto saxophone for you." I fully agree with him about buying that baseball glove; I wasn't so sure about the saxophone. I didn't miss eating out at restaurants because never having had that experience, I had no idea what I was missing. My mother was a great cook, so eating at home was just fine with me, the only exception being that rare opportunity to devour one of those White Castle hamburgers. It's true we seldom if ever ate in restaurants; however, my dad did break our family dining routine about once every two months in an interesting way. He would go to the downtown farmers market and bring home a live chicken for my mother to cook. It was an exciting time to see him place the chicken's neck on a wood post in the backyard then snip the head off with one sharp stroke of his ax. Blood would squirt all over, and, to my dismay, the chicken would run around with no head. Let me tell you, I stood well behind my dad when this exciting event occurred. It was a frightening experience, but the chicken and dumpling dinner that followed was worth being scared out of my wits!

On a more positive note, every once in a while my dad and I would drive to downtown Saint Paul to the New Kin Chew Chinese restaurant. He would request a large takeout order of chow mein. This had to be the most delicious chow mein I have ever eaten. There are loads of Chinese restaurants in our community today, but only one can compare with the taste of chow mein from the New Kin Chew restaurant. Try eating at the Dragon Cafe in Shakopee, Minnesota, and you will understand what I mean. All those other Chinese restaurants should take lessons from the Dragon Cafe; they must have gotten the recipe from New Kin Chew!

It's only fair that I mention we did spend our key holidays having dinner at both of my grandparents' and my aunt's home; of course, they were freebies! I am sure there were many fine restaurants in our community in those days, but I suspect my folks figured they were there for those rich folks living on Summit Avenue or residing in Highland Park's silk stocking neighborhood. Thank God, my mother was a great cook. To put it simply, eating out was a luxury that my folks and most of their friends and relatives simply couldn't afford. In the 1930s there were other far more important needs that required cash, even for those folks fortunate enough to have a job. The exception would be that dime I needed for "you know what"! Today, eating out is viewed by many to be an everyday experience. Just check the local restaurants on a weekend night, and most are filled to the rafters. A friend recently told me his wife was a lousy cook, so eating out was a necessity. He failed to check that blank on his premarital checklist. So I'll say it again, eating out in the 1930s was viewed as an absolute luxury, considered by most folks to be a frivolous use of cash; today it is an everyday experience with little concern for cost. Check your monthly credit card report listing restaurants you frequented, and you may be surprised!

Smoking/Drinking Cheap

In the 1930s and 1940s, smoking seemed to be a high priority ... almost as important as eating. Just about every man and many women smoked either cigarettes, a pipe, or one of those smelly cigars. Cigarette companies would give out free small cigarette packages at the Lexington baseball park to everyone, even kids. That billboard on the third base grandstand wall stated in big letters, "Walk a Mile for a Camel," a popular cigarette brand. In those days smoking was just a way of life. Many fellows decided to "roll their own" to save on the cost of a pack of cigarettes. It was far cheaper to buy tobacco in a pouch and to roll your own cigarettes. To quit smoking and save a buck was pretty much out of the question, so rolling your own was an inexpensive alternative. When it came to drinking booze, if the good stuff was too expensive, a cheap bottle of "Ripple" might just be the solution—if it didn't kill you!

Transportation Was a Luxury

When you didn't have wheels readily available it was necessary to be innovative and try to come up with an alternative mobility source. If you couldn't afford a horse, a car, or even the token for a streetcar ride around town, you had to be resourceful. Walking was the number one solution, but to own a bicycle (if you could afford one) was even a better solution. Having to travel a distance for a job (if you could find one) or to attend school a few miles away without some form of transportation could really put you behind the eight ball. To own a car was a luxury, but in many cases a necessity if you wanted to work. In 1938 my dad handed the salesman at Midway Chevrolet $800 in cold hard cash to purchase a new Chevrolet. He said, "If I'm going to fix cars for a living, I'm sure as heck going to own one, and I'm not going to pay the bank a nickel of interest, and I'll also do my own car repairs. Why pay the Chevrolet repair garage for oil changes and other repairs when I can do it myself?" He proceeded to dig out about a five- by three-foot pit in the center of our garage, which he built. He constructed a small ladder to climb in and out of this pit. After driving his car over this pit, he would then crawl under the car, climb down the ladder and do the repair work; fortunately the cars in those days were built high off the ground. Oh, yes, he used the drain oil taken from the cars in the repair shop where he

15

worked for his car oil. It didn't cost him a nickel, so he had free oil changes for the eight years he owned this car. After this experience, he considered Chevrolet the best car on the market because the maintenance never cost him a dime. My dad was a Chevrolet junkie for life. By the way, after owning this Chevrolet for eight years, he handed it off to my brother. After my brother wore it out, and it needed repairs, it ended in my lap. I finished it off!

In the 1930s I was fortunate to own what you might call a striped-down bike that lacked all those fancy accessories. There was this neighbor kid who owned a fancy Schwinn bike with handle bar brakes, a speedometer, and lights on the front and back fender, and it could be shifted into three different speeds. This bike was the envy of every kid in the neighborhood. We all figured this kid was rich and kind of gave him the cold shoulder. You guessed right; we were jealous of him. Years later at our high school class reunion, I met this neighbor fellow and told him how we would have given anything to have wealthy parents so we could have owned a bike like his. He said, "You guys had it all wrong. We weren't rich; my uncle won this bike in a contest and gave it to me for my birthday." I guess he wasn't such a bad kid after all!

When you don't have "wheels" readily available, one solution is to piggyback on someone who already has wheels. The solution was very simple. It was called hitchhiking. You simply stood on the corner and put your hand out (with your thumb up) in the direction you wanted to go and patiently waited for a friendly motorist who felt sorry for you. Hitchhiking was really common during the 1930s, so I decided to join the group and began using this means of getting around town from the time I was eight years old. It was the simplest and cheapest way to get downtown, to visit my friends across town, to go swimming, to get to school and get to just about anywhere. It was not uncommon in the 1940s for me to hitchhike to my jobs, to meet my girlfriend for a date, or to travel to my out-of-town baseball games. My mom and dad had no objection to this unique means of transportation and encouraged it; after all, they didn't have to provide me gas money or pay for streetcar tokens! The biggest hurdle to hitchhiking was arriving at a street corner when there were two or three other fellows hitchhiking at this same corner. The solution to that problem was to sneak a couple blocks in front of them and catch a ride before the car that picked you up reached their corner. It wasn't the best way to make friends, but all's fair in love and transportation!

In all the years of hitchhiking, I remember only one problem. I picked up a ride by the Como Park golf course and was heading south on Lexington Avenue when another car cut right in front of the car I was riding in, barely avoiding an accident. My driver got hot as a pistol, and a few blocks down the road swerved directly in front of this car cutting him off. My driver jumped out of the car and headed for this other car. There was trouble brewing. It was road rage in action! I quietly slipped out of the rider's side and left the scene as fast as my legs would carry me. Frankly, I wasn't in the fighting mood. I hailed another car for a ride a few blocks away and never did find out who got the first punch in. Hitchhiking was comparable to an unscheduled airline. When the budget for transportation was zero, it provided an excellent alternative for arriving at one's destination ... sometimes early but more often late. It proved there was more than one way to skin a cat (my dad's favorite saying) when owning a car, horse, bike, or any other vehicle was low priority on the budget scale. I found people in general to be very nice and helpful. More than once, when I hitched a ride on Lexington Avenue by Lake Como to get to school, the driver would deviate from his schedule and go six blocks out of the way to drop me off right at the school's front door. Hitchhiking at 2:30 a.m. from Madeline's Ice Cream Parlor on Snelling Avenue, where my girlfriend worked, to my home in the Como neighborhood was a far greater challenge; a few times it ended up being a long walk. In addition to gaining cheap transportation, hitchhiking also offered a wonderful opportunity to meet new people, to gain a passenger seat education, and to ride in some really classy cars.

Fancy Travel

In the 1930s the only commercial means of travel I can remember was via the Greyhound bus. You would board the bus at the downtown bus station and travel to any exotic destination in the country. That Greyhound bus took you just about anywhere you wanted to go. We rarely left town, and if we traveled anywhere it was in my dad's 1938 Chevrolet. I figured taking a Greyhound bus, which cost money, was only for those rich folks with cash who loved to travel. Whenever I saw one of those Greyhound buses traveling down the road, I remember thinking how exciting it would be to be a passenger heading to some unknown but exotic destination. It really didn't cost anything to dream. I later discovered riding the bus wasn't that exciting a ride after all; the airplane offered a much bigger thrill!

Those yellow school buses so prevalent today were nowhere to be found in the 1930s, except in some remote rural areas. There simply was no category in city school district budgets in those years titled "transportation." Today it's a multi-million-dollar operation. If it was too far to walk, ride a bike, or have someone drive you to school, you most likely didn't attend school. The school dropout rate during those Depression years was excessive as you can imagine, in addition to the large percentage of children and young adults who decided they simply didn't need an education. It made sense; if you had to travel a distance to attend school, and there was no means of transportation, you probably registered for the school of "hard knocks," requiring no tuition! It should be pointed out, however, that school attendance in the 1930s was not valued as highly as it is today.

There were many instances where working on the farm was considered more important than attending school. Many farmers figured that education wasn't really necessary if their sons were going to be farmers the rest of their lives. For many families, even in the cities, it was easy to justify not attending school if the distance to school was excessive. The availability of school busing today makes education pretty much a mandatory requirement for all children. Maybe this is why busing is so low on the popularity scale for certain students, and is highly popular with so many parents!

I well remember Tommy, a classmate who attended school until the fifth grade and was never seen again. He had some obvious learning problems, and I expect he was tired of being the black sheep in the class. There was no adaption by the teacher to meet his special needs, and no effort was made to return him to school. Today an outreach staff member would be sent to his home making sure he would return to school and most likely be placed in a special education class. After all, the school district could well use that additional $6,000 of student foundation aid. There were no classes for special needs students in those days. If you couldn't keep up with the regular classroom work, you just fell behind, which led to this excessive dropout rate. Today special education services are mandated by federal legislation for all special needs students. Just try and drop out today; they will catch you and drag you back!

Apparently receiving an education was high on my folks' priority list because the only excuse for me not attending school was when I came down with some dreaded disease that would infect others. I remember the doctor using that infamous word *contagious*. When I had the measles, and a few years later, impetigo, I remember being forced to stay home in bed having that yellow Health Department sign hanging outside the front door to keep all visitors away. Having a cold, a headache, or fear of an upcoming test were simply not valid excuses to avoid school. There were a few times I tried faking having the measles so I could stay home, but it was hard to fool my mother with no spots on my face. It did cross my mind at the time that maybe my mother's primary concern wasn't so much my getting an education but simply wanting me out of the house for some peace and quiet.

The Catholic grade school I attended did have a school hot lunch service, but that cost money. Initially I carried a bag lunch to school like so many of my friends. After I got a bike, I would ride that six blocks home for lunch and hustle back. My mom always had something special. It would have been easier to purchase that school hot lunch, but it was an additional expense added to the Catholic school tuition package. Frankly, the school hot lunches weren't as good as the lunch my mom prepared except when spanish rice was on the school lunch menu. I just loved it and could smell it cooking as I passed by the cafeteria on the way to my bike. My mom just never made that great spanish rice. The nuns would give us a pitch on offering up to God something we really liked; I guess for me, being a good Catholic, it was that delicious spanish rice!

A Child of the Times

During those tremulous 1930s, there was a famous saying that "children should be seen and not heard." In other words, parents were in charge at home, and teachers were in charge at school. Us kids were in charge of nothing! If you had trouble at school, you faced double trouble: punishment at school and even more severe repercussions to follow at home. Spanking wasn't banned in the 1930s! During those Depression years, there were far more important things to worry about than a problem kid, so a good spanking was much more popular than the current counseling approach. Parents were in charge, period, and not the child! Some younger folks reading this book may not understand this theory at all. I hesitate to admit it, but to be perfectly honest, I was a shy kid with little confidence and certainly not a troublemaker. I was not out to challenge my folks, especially my no-nonsense German father. Also at this early age I unfortunately was a bed-wetter, which kept me close to home and seriously limited my outings and any overnights with relatives and friends. I'm not sure if the effects of the Depression and my bed-wetting had anything to do with my shyness and lack of confidence but wouldn't be surprised if they did. I think my folks' worries about what was happening in our country may well have rubbed off on me and added to my shyness. When school began, certain events occurred in my life that apparently brought me out of my shell into the real world. There is nothing like a little success to make you feel you might be just as good as all those other kids.

I vividly recall my grandfather carrying me screaming and kicking to his car when he drove me to my very first day of kindergarten. Apparently I felt it was safer to stay home protected by my mother. This negative behavior attracted little attention, so I reluctantly decided on the second day to walk to school with the other kids. It didn't take long to realize that I was going to get an education whether I wanted it or not. Two events occurred in my elementary school days that opened my eyes to the fact I wasn't just another boring kid but had some skills that upped my self-confidence level! Our grade school had an excellent baseball team, and when I reached the sixth grade, I was eligible to play. I decided to avoid trying out for this team figuring I wasn't good enough. My dad felt different and forced me to attend that first practice. Well, as a sixth-grader, to my surprise I ended up being the team's starting pitcher. That same year there was a music contest held at one of Saint Paul's large high schools. My dad registered me in the saxophone contest. I absolutely refused to participate and cried my eyes out when he forced me to attend. Wouldn't you know, I won first prize and a nice gold-plated medal. My dad's persistence helped change my life, and these successes gave me more confidence to face life's challenges.

Although the Depression was certainly a negative experience for almost everyone, my dad showed me that out of darkness, there still can be light. That's a lesson I will carry to the grave.

Just Getting By

My dad's father died when he was seven years old, so at that very early age he was expected to work and contribute to the family's income. He quit school after the sixth grade and assisted his mother in their small confectionery store. At about age fourteen he went to work at the Auto Engine Works Company learning on the job to be a machinist. He worked six days a week at this job making automobile parts earning a very marginal wage. He fortunately was employed, while so many of our neighbors and relatives were unemployed. He later began working in the mid-1930s as a mechanic for the Saint Paul Fire Department Repair Shop. The wages again were minimal, but he felt that working for the City of Saint Paul was a more stable position with some important fringe benefits. Security was the name of the game in his mind, and he often stressed this fact to me as I became of working age. Any type of city, state, or federal civil service job was high on my dad's priority list because of the security these jobs offered; the salary amount was secondary. My dad shared with me in later life that a family picnic outing was really his primary source of enjoyment and entertainment as a youngster. He said that dropping out of school in the sixth grade to go to work cut him out of any opportunities for athletics and social events. That probably explains why after supper my dad would hand me my baseball glove, and we would play catch by the hour. I think he enjoyed it as much as I did. He wanted me to have all the opportunities he never had. I honestly believe his goal was for me to become a great left-handed pitcher just like Johnny VanderMeer, who hurled two no-hitters for the Cincinnati Reds in the early 1940s. (Well, at least I did become a decent but not great left-handed pitcher). My grandfather, who lived next door to us, thought playing baseball was a complete waste of time. I think he figured everyone should be working all the time. Years later when I received a paycheck for playing baseball, I understand he changed his mind. My grandpa just didn't understand talent when he saw it!

Even though money was tight, my parents saw to it that both my brother and I had music lessons. I was seven years old when we checked the want ads for a used saxophone for me and a used trumpet for my brother. Our music teacher, Mr. Paul Lau, was a cello player in the Minneapolis Symphony orchestra. I suspect this outstanding professional musician was earning poverty wages, if any wages, from the orchestra during those tough financial times and was supplementing his income by giving lessons. What a comedown for this featured professional musician to give beginning lessons to two untalented kids. I never found out what these lessons cost, but I'm sure it didn't exceed a dollar a lesson. In those challenging 1930s, beggars couldn't be choosy—even professional musicians! Apparently, my brother found those music lessons a little more challenging than me because Mr. Lau more than once would say, "Vernon, you play this exercise so your brother can see how it should be played." My brother was two years older than me, and to show him up was a real thrill, but not for my brother. He would give me that evil look that was his way of saying, "I'll deal with you later!" Frankly, it made my day. Anyway, I could run faster than him.

Our family lived in a small three-bedroom home my dad had built in Saint Paul's Midway District right next door to his parents. I understand his parents owned this lot and gifted it to him. He had to get city approval to build this home because the lot was narrow and didn't meet city building codes. My folks occupied one bedroom, and my brother and I slept on bunk beds my dad had made, in the second tiny bedroom. Our roomer (yes, we had a roomer) lived in the third bedroom. We all shared the one bathroom and managed to somehow get by. Mr. Enter, our first roomer, worked in downtown Saint Paul. I understand he was trying to make enough money to bring his family over to America from Austria. When he moved out, Mr. Lennon moved in. He was a barber and lived with us for quite a few years. This extra income was very beneficial as a supplement to my dad's marginal salary. On the other hand, it was beneficial to both our roomers because their monthly rent was far less then residing in a rooming house or hotel. Privacy didn't seem much of an issue back then, adding to the family income, however, was an important issue. I never thought of it at the time, but I wouldn't be surprised if my folks used that extra rent money to pay for our music lessons and for those baseballs I failed to catch that ended up in the city sewer system. In time, my throwing and catching skills did improve, so I no longer had to crawl down the sewer at our street corner to retrieve those dirty, wet baseballs. By the way, because baseballs were expensive, we would use them till the leather cover fell off and then tape them up for further use. Believe me, there was no waste in those days!

During the Depression, with money so scarce, most women were skilled at sewing and made and repaired much of the family clothing. My wife's mother sewed all of her underclothing and dresses in her early years. In her high school years, she purchased most of her clothing from the bargain basement at Montgomery Ward's, which was just a few blocks from her home. Believe me, Ward's bargain basement was a very popular location. In talking to many retired farmers' wives, I learned that it was very popular to convert those flour sacks with pretty designs into dresses for their daughters and underwear for the boys. As a youngster, I knew what I would be wearing in the next year or two by observing what my brother was wearing. "Hand-me-downs" was the name of the game. I'll always remember my folks checking the clothing want ads in the *Saint Paul Dispatch* paper. My dad said it was important to check the addresses of these clothing ads. He was only interested in contacting those homes in Saint Paul's classy neighborhoods where you would find the best clothes. That slick sport coat I picked out for just a few dollars from that fancy home in Highland Park was almost too nice to wear. My friends never knew or cared that my clothes were nearly all secondhand because most of their clothes were secondhand or thirdhand as well!

Homemaker—A Full-Time Occupation

I remember asking my mother, during a visit to her retirement center, why as a registered nurse she didn't secure a nursing job during those Depression years when money was so tight. She said, "Are you kidding? My relatives and friends would have disowned me if I had gone to work. Married women with children in those days were expected to be 'homemakers,' and the husband's job was to make the living. To be perfectly honest, doing all those tedious homemaker tasks and raising you kids was a full-time job and more." She went on to say, "I loved being a nurse and would have enjoyed working longer after your dad and I were married, but as soon as the hospital learned of my pregnancy, I was terminated." This was interesting because in 1953 my wife was also immediately terminated from her bookkeeping job the day her boss discovered she was pregnant. Apparently, this company policy to terminate women when they became pregnant was common practice all during those Depression years and for many years after as well. Wow, what would have happened to this country if women would have balked at becoming pregnant? One thing for sure, a bunch of us old-timers wouldn't be around to talk about it. I'm at a loss as to why being pregnant would affect a woman's work performance. It certainly didn't affect the performance of that pregnant weather lady on the ten o'clock TV news who a month ago had her baby at 2:00 a.m. immediately following her broadcast.

In those dire 1930s, as my mother stated, she was employed full time in a nonpaying job, seven days a week that involved more hours of labor then my dad's ten-hour workday, with no vacation days. This was that job entitled "homemaker." She possessed relatively few of those fancy time-saving home appliances that are present in all homes today. It was all "do it by hand" work. I remember Monday was always washing clothes day, which literally took all day. She would sort out all the dirty clothes, place them in our electric washing machine, then wring each clothes item out using the ringer device located on top of the washing machine. She then put a bluing product in the washing machine and proceeded to wash the white clothes again, run them through the ringer the second time, then placed them in our laundry tub filled with clean water and squished them around with a big stick to remove the soap. She ran them through the ringer the third time before leaving the basement and hung all the clothes on the rope laundry line that was permanently present in the backyard. Once wind dried, she would place the clothes into the laundry basket and sort and fold them to be put away. Certain clothes needed ironing, which took almost as much time as the washing process. In the meantime, she had three meals to make but generally left the dusting and cleaning chores to another day. Most folks we knew didn't have this fancy electric washing machine and did all their clothes scrubbing by hand using that fancy washboard. With the modern washing and drying machines in each home today, this can hardly be considered a time-consuming job, while it was an all-day job back in the 1930s.

My folks were fortunate to have a gas stove, and each burner was lit with a match. Our next-door neighbor had a wood-burning stove, as did many of our other neighbors. If you didn't have electricity or gas available, that wood stove was a necessity. Remember, in the 1930s many rural communities and farms had yet to be hooked up with electricity. Those fancy ovens and microwaves present today were still in the dreamer stage. You can see where cooking, baking, and canning were very time-consuming tasks. Our mothers baked bread a minimum of two days a week, and canning food was a way of life. I can still picture those rows of mason jars filled with corn, beans, and other delicacies lining the shelf in that special room in the basement where those food items were stored. In those communities and on farms where refrigeration was unavailable, meat products were also canned and stored in the coolest location in the basement. George, the iceman, brought a block of ice to our home and placed it in our icebox on a regular basis. Fresh milk with that cream on top was also delivered to our home by a milkman, who placed the milk bottles just outside our back door. It was my job to transfer them to the icebox.

This homemaker position was more than a full-time job. After my brother and I were in high school, my mother decided to reopen her nursing career by working in a local hospital two evenings a week. Her female friends and relatives rose up in arms chastising her for ever considering leaving her full-time homemaking job. On the other hand, we considered her a true pioneer. How different than in today's world, where women are criticized if they don't hold down a paying job plus being a homemaker.

Cheap Recreation

Let me share with you what a person could do for excitement without spending a fortune. You could attend a Saint Paul Saints professional baseball game and sit in the bleachers by joining the Saints knothole gang for the sum of ten cents. The cheapest way to sit in the main grandstand, however, was to arrive at the game early and stand outside the park attempting to retrieve a batting practice foul ball or home run over the fence. This was a competitive task, but if you were lucky and retrieved the ball and returned it to the groundskeeper, you were rewarded a free ticket to the game. In those early days, every effort was made by teams to retrieve baseballs and to reuse them—dirty, marked up, or even slightly damaged. They were considered a valuable, very expensive item (over two dollars a ball). Today baseballs seem to have little value. Players routinely throw them to the fans, and absolutely no effort is made to retrieve foul balls. By the way, if there is just a slight mark on a baseball today, it is tossed out to be used later only for batting practice. Gosh, maybe the teams get them free today!

As kids we organized our own ball games, purchased our own equipment, made up our own rules, and played games without adult direction, and had fun doing it. There was no paid recreational director organizing our activities, and our parents seldom attended our unorganized games and other activities because they had other more important things to do. We didn't have organized teams until our teen years, and then trophies were given only to the championship team. Recently a friend of mine told me his son's team didn't win a baseball game but received a trophy for being the best losers. They celebrated by accepting this trophy at the local Dairy Queen restaurant where parents bought them Blizzards for this wonderful accomplishment. Gosh, once I was invited to a player's home for Kool-Aid and cookies when we won the championship. Apparently, we were born fifty years too soon!

If you wanted to attend the traveling Ringling Brothers Circus or decided to attend the Minnesota State Fair, you would show up at Circus Hill in Saint Paul or to the fairgrounds just before setup time. You would be hired on the spot to help them unpack and construct the tents or midway rides. The reward was those wonderful free tickets. I don't plan to share the secret my friends and I followed to sneak each day into the state fair when our free tickets were used up. You also should know that the Saint Paul Winter Carnival Parade and many carnival activities were free to attend, and the Como Park Zoo and concerts in the Como Park Pavilion were also free. Skating on Como Lake and playing or watching baseball or football games on Dunning Field didn't cost a nickel. If you were clever, and in some instances willing to take a chance, there was no lack of fun activities that were free. To attend certain events might entail being a bit sneaky and the ability to run fast when chased!

Community/Government Help

In the 1930s, the primary agency to offer help for families in need was the County Welfare Office. This agency was underfunded and basically able to aid only the most severe indigent families. Certain church settings offered help to selected parishioners, but when it came right down to it, the primary source of assistance to people in need was when families helped families. When my grandfather died, my elderly grandmother moved in with my folks for four months, then to Marshfield, Wisconsin, to live with another daughter for four months. She then moved to California and lived with another daughter for four months, and then back with my folks to begin the cycle again. This seemed like a good living solution for my grandmother—family taking care of family. Years later, after my dad died, I offered my mother the opportunity to live in the lower-level apartment of our home so she could save on expenses and have us close by. She thanked me for this invitation but declined saying, "I'm not going to ruin your life!" This arrangement with my grandmother may have been cost effective for my parents but apparently resulted in a few emotional scars. This was something my mother was going to avoid by not living with us. It makes me wonder what my children's reaction would be if I asked to live with them in my final years. I'm not sure I want to know!

Speaking of grandparents, as a kid I was fortunate to have the grandparents on my dad's side living right next door to our home. My grandmother had remarried in later life, and with a limited income they couldn't afford the luxury of a phone, so my dad rigged up a buzzer system between our home and their home. When someone called our phone asking to talk to grandma, my mother would press the buzzer, and grandma would hustle over to our house and receive her call. Years later, when my elderly mother was living in her retirement residence, we talked about this economical communication system. My mother said, "It may have saved Grandma some money, but it was a terrible system. Grandma would come over and never go home!" I guess there are times when saving a buck just isn't worth it.

There were relatively few residential living settings available for the elderly during those Depression years. Most nursing homes were for the sick and those in need of medical assistance, and were not set up for the more capable senior citizens. I do recall a large building on Saint Paul's east side that was called the "Poor Farm." There was also the "Old Soldiers Home" for indigent older gentlemen who had served in the military service. Residences for elderly citizens were few and costly. These residences were basically available to the well to do and were beyond the financial reach of most working-class Americans. The retirement residences that are blossoming throughout the country today were simply a dream in those days. Many of the indigent older folks with no family or other resources ended up living on the streets and eating at soup kitchens or eating what could be scrounged from restaurant throwaways. It was not uncommon to be stopped by folks pleading for a handout. You know, it's frustrating to provide someone with a dime for a cup of coffee when you don't have the dime!

The banks that had closed and those that later reopened were stingy when it came to making loans without secure collateral, which few people had. To put it bluntly, banks were practically useless for those folks with no jobs or for marginal workers with no savings or assets of any kind. In short, you were on your own to survive in a country that was at a standstill. It was the time when a few innovative people thought making one's own paper money might be a profitable business to consider. Unfortunately, some used the wrong-color paper. That's when the word *paperhanging* was coined by the police as their favorite term to describe folks who felt making their own money was a valid business. It was an innovative business idea but a bit risky. I don't think those wealthy *Shark Tank* panelists would have been interested in investing their money with a company that wanted to make "pretend" money!

Some folks unhappy with their lack of spending money in the 1930s attempted a new, quite exciting, occupation entitled, "robbing banks." It was a quick way of gaining wealth and enjoying the good life but slightly on the illegal side. One of the more notorious bank robbers was a gentleman who carried out this occupation in Chicago and spent time in Saint Paul to "cool off" between jobs. Fortunately for him, Saint Paul's chief of police was well paid off to protect him from the authorities with the understanding that Mr. Dillinger would agree to be a model citizen while residing in Saint Paul. In time, he met his fate by a Chicago policeman's submachine gun. My dad would always point out his "cooling off" residence on Lexington Avenue in Saint Paul. Apparently, Mr. Dillinger was quite a popular figure in town. This "thinking out of the box" approach to making money was highly discouraged by most crime-fighting agencies.

The government developed a program entitled the Civilian Conservation Corps (CCC) that would offer some semblance of work for young adult males. This program offered work to thousands of unemployed young men in work projects that included the development and upgrading of state and national parks plus numerous other projects to enhance environmental needs in the country. Many examples of CCC work projects can still be viewed today when visiting both our Minnesota state parks and the boundary waters area, and in the federal park system. An even larger work program arranged through the government was titled Work Progress Administration (WPA). This program was another attempt to keep thousands of America's working-aged folks, especially men, employed in meaningful jobs. Their work projects included building roads, roadside rest areas, selected buildings, and local park and recreation improvements. Many of these projects can be viewed right in our own state of Minnesota even today. An example of WPA work to be viewed locally in Minnesota would include the construction of Highway 100, many of the roadside rest stops located next to major highways, selected buildings at the State Fairgrounds in Saint Paul, and innumerable building projects in our Twin Cities parks. The pay received from these government work programs was minimal, but it served the purpose of keeping many working-age men active and involved in productive tasks. The use of heavy machinery in these projects was kept to a minimum to keep as many men employed as possible. Picks and shovels were the tools of the day.

My dad told me about a friend of his who joined one of these work programs constructing the Alaskan Highway in the 1930s. There was no work locally, so he decided to join this Alaskan construction project with plans to save enough money to build a home when he returned to Minnesota. Unfortunately the poker games and booze drained him of his cash, and he returned home empty-handed. My dad said his friends and family were thoroughly disgusted with him when he returned home with less money than when he left. Years later my folks and our family attended a band concert at the Lake Como Pavilion. When the concert was over, my dad introduced me to the band's lead trumpet player. On our way home he explained that this was the same fellow who lost all the money he had earned in Alaska and returned empty-handed. He said, "You know, sometimes surviving adversity can be life's best teacher because on his return home he quit drinking, got married, had a family, found a steady job, and is enjoying this music hobby." My dad's comment about surviving adversity is so true, not only for this fellow but for all those folks who managed to survive the challenge of that Great Depression. By the way, you also can expect to face adversity in some way or another in your lifetime, and how you handle it may well dictate your future. Let this trumpet player be your example!

Getting Double-Teamed

If living through a dormant economy wasn't enough, farmers were facing an additional problem. A very destructive drought occurred in the 1930s that made it nearly impossible to raise crops. In many areas of the Midwest, the extremely dry topsoil would be picked up by the winds, resulting in severe dust storms, making farming almost impossible. This was labeled the Dust Bowl and resulted in many farmers leaving their farms in desperation, while those who remained were living under dire conditions. A retired farmer in our retirement center tells how many farmers receiving financial aid under the Federal Land Grant Program were unable to make their annual payment, which would normally result in foreclosure procedures. He said the government had little interest in getting stuck with this land, so it simply forgave these unpaid loans and allowed the farmers to remain on their land. My mother had a nursing school friend who married a farmer in the Saint Cloud area, and in the summer of 1938 our family decided to visit their farm. Some twenty minutes after we arrived, my mother told my dad we had to leave. She said these folks didn't have enough food for their own family, let alone ours. She used some excuse for not staying, and we were on our way. I was told by more than one retired farmer in my retirement residence that times were so tough in the mid-'30s that some farmers were forced to shoot their cattle because there was no feed available. Just think, they were killing off their livelihood. It wasn't only farmers that were affected by these negative weather conditions. I have seen pictures of Prior Lake in 1934, where we resided for many years, and was shocked to see crops growing on the lake area behind our home where today the water height is fourteen inches. Those pictures showed simply two puddles of water in what today is the center of the lake. How challenging for those folks who owned lake property and for those farmers who had their income source negatively affected by both the poor economy and this severe drought. And we complain about rain at a family picnic!

Thinking out of the Box

In those difficult times, the family breadwinner was left with the choice of aggressively fighting for any job to be found or in absolute desperation joining those long lines at the soup kitchen. There were many industrious folks, however, who were not willing to give up without a fight and who viewed this unemployment problem as an opportunity to try something different. They were willing to try an alternative approach ... explore a new idea ... to "think out of the box." I asked a good friend of mine how his family's very successful produce business ever got started during the Depression. He explained that his dad had a truck garden, but local folks couldn't afford to pay the price for his produce. One day, in desperation, he decided to try a new sales approach. He loaded his old model T truck with as much produce as it could handle and proceeded to travel that one-hundred-plus-mile journey to Duluth, Minnesota. He drove down to the Lake Superior boat yards with his goods. He sold every single item he had in his truck to the cooks on the boats that shipped iron ore out of the Duluth harbor. They were impressed with the quality of his produce and told him they would purchase everything he could deliver to them. From that day on, he proceeded to make two trips a day to Duluth in that rickety old truck and sold everything he could grow. He eventually purchased a better truck, and his business prospered. He continued to expand, and today his company operates a highly successful nationwide produce business. He didn't quit gardening and give up; he was willing to explore something new. His new approach paid off because he was willing to "think out of the box"! You know, sometimes the Hail Mary pass in football really works. My friend's dad threw that Hail Mary pass, and it went for a touchdown in Duluth!

My dad tightened his belt and tried every possible way to save a buck and keep out of debt. For example, he didn't pay to have his trash hauled away but instead burned it in the burn pit he built in his backyard. He refused to waste a dime on trash haulers when he could dispose of his trash for nothing. He absolutely loved strawberries, so instead of buying them from the store, he grew strawberries in a barrel placed in our backyard. He picked up an old whiskey barrel, drilled holes in the side of the barrel, filled it with dirt, and proceeded to plant strawberries in those holes. It was a great idea, but unfortunately the birds ate the strawberries before he did. Trial and error ... sometimes things work out, and then sometimes they don't. To save a few bucks, my dad made some of the furniture in our home. I especially remember our bunk beds that were made of solid maple. These bunk beds were unscratchable, bulky, and heavy but are still being used by our grandchildren. He bought his clothes from Jake's, a Jewish clothing store in Minneapolis where you could barter down the price. He loved to barter with the store clerk on pricing, and I don't believe he ever paid the listed price. His motto was, "Never buy anything you can build yourself, and never pay the listed price for anything," and he meant anything! Decent toys in those days were expensive, so with the help of my brother, they built motorized chugs, which resembled small racing cars, that we drove all over the neighborhood. Believe me, no other kids had toys that matched ours. He was always willing to try something different or to explore a new idea. Some folks considered my dad cheap, but they were wrong; he was smart but frugal. I love that word, *frugal*!

As challenging as those economic times were in 1939, my dad had set his mind on attending the World's Fair being held in New York City that year. The theme of this fair offered a prediction of what America would be like in the year 1960. My dad wanted to view firsthand this futuristic picture of America and for his family to share this view as well. The challenge was how to finance such a trip in those trying times. He knew that flying or traveling by bus was far too expensive and realized that getting around New York City would require a car. He decided the only way to take this trip was to drive to New York City and back in our 1938 Chevrolet, realizing there were few motels, restaurants, gas stations, and absolutely no freeways as there are today. This trip meant driving right through the heart of Chicago, Detroit, and Cleveland, making this a long, tiring trip. To save money, he decided to stay in private homes instead of hotels, and instead of eating in restaurants, we would purchase food from grocery stores and eat along the road. Through friends he arranged for us to stay in a private home in Flushing, New York, while attending the fair. To cover the cost of gas, he agreed to take one of our friends along as a guest. The guest's parents paid for all their son's expenses plus the cost of gas.

Five of us piled into our 1938 Chevrolet, had a long and at times laboring trip but viewed an exciting world's fair and saw all those amazing sights of New York City. Most of our relatives said such a trip was too dangerous, couldn't be done, and would cost a fortune. Others said it was an impossible trip. My dad fooled them all by taking a chance and providing our family with the adventure of a lifetime! He proved that most anything is possible if you are willing to "think out of the box" and try a new approach to achieve your dream. He set a wonderful example for my brother and me. I recall him saying more than once, "There's always a way. Just put your mind to work!"

CHAPTER 3

Can History Teach Us Anything?

What does all this talk about the Great Depression have to do with having a successful work career or retirement in today's world? Well, I believe it has everything to do with it. Have you noticed lately all those old, white-haired senior citizens driving around in their fancy convertibles? How about the number of old folks living in expensive retirement residences that are springing up all over the country? Are you aware of those many senior citizens that can afford to spend their winters in beautiful Phoenix, balmy Florida, and in the Texas Valley? It's an interesting fact that most old codgers in their mideighties (including this author) were raised during this depression period and personally experienced those financially challenging times. These folks who lived through those dire times learned how to squeeze a nickel and never forgot those frugal survival tips that led them to their retirement rocking chair, and to cash to buy that fancy convertible. Believe me, those experiences on how to survive with limited cash are hard to forget. They are ingrained right in our bones. I honestly believe it's almost a genetic thing!

I know there are a few of my friends and even members of my family that would probably label me "cheap." I'd prefer my dad's term: *frugal*. Don't you think *frugal* has a more professional ring to it? I'm proud of my parents' frugality and the practical lessons they taught me that have remained indelibly in my mind over the years. Label me whatever you like, but I'm able to drive a paid-for brand new car with a sunroof (I've graduated from convertibles), live in a beautiful retirement residence, and vacation every winter in Mexico. And, oh yes, this is important, I never made a six-figure income. I smile when I tell people, "Everything I know, I learned from surviving the Great Depression." Understand from the start that any advice and suggestions recorded in this book originate back to the conservative life skills I picked up in those first twelve years of my life. Thanks, Mom and Dad, for giving me that Economics 101 course on being cheap. I'm sorry; I mean being frugal!

Our grandparents and parents who lived through the Depression followed three key principles of survival that made it possible for them to enjoy their retirement. By the way, these principles are the basis for my dad's mythical Economics 101 course. They are really very simple: (1) stay out of debt, (2) always save something, and (3) don't give your money away. A fourth principle I'd like to add is a willingness to be innovative, or, better stated, be willing to "think out of the box." My dad always saved something even if it was fifty cents, and he religiously paid his bills in full using cash. There were a few instances when he did charge at our neighborhood Schiller's grocery store but never failed to pay the full bill at the end of each month. He refused to go in debt and never purchased a major item if he didn't have the cash. I don't think he ever owned or even thought of using a credit card till the day he died. The 1938 Chevrolet he purchased for $800 was a cash deal. I wonder if he would have paid cash for that $60,000 pickup truck I recently saw advertised on TV? Knowing my dad, I think he would have more likely paid cash for that 2004 used Chevy pickup truck advertised in the Minneapolis newspaper want ads for $5,000, with his final offer being $4,000 and not a cent more! These four principles, maybe with a few adaptations, are just as valuable in today's world as they were in the 1930s if an enjoyable lifestyle, working career, and eventual retirement are on your "bucket list."

I'll be the first to admit that times have radically changed from those infamous 1930s to today's world. No one expects young folks in 2018 to start hitchhiking, buying clothes at Jake's, or riding those railroad boxcars from town to town … although it sounds like fun! It's up to each individual to come up with his or her own solution to survive economically in the current fast-paced computerized society where low wages, high inflation, and challenges too numerous to mention abound. It's this author's contention, however, that those key principles my grandparents and parents lived by still hold true in today's world:

1. Stay out of debt.
2. Always save something.
3. Don't give your money away.
4. Be willing to "think out of the box."

I almost forgot to add the word *sacrifice* to those lists of principles. Remember that old saying, "If something is easy, anyone can do it; if it's hard, only a few will try." Or better yet, "Sacrifice today, and enjoy tomorrow."

CHAPTER 4

When the World Changed

On December 7, 1941, the entire world changed! The Depression abruptly came to a halt when the Japanese attacked Pearl Harbor and the Second World War started with a huge bang. All the eligible able-bodied young men quickly enlisted in the services of our country. Men and women of all ages capable of employment entered the working force in masses to aid in the war effort. No more soup kitchens, the "hobo" era vanished, no more long unemployment lines, and the attitude of the country overnight had transformed from depression and futility to a renewed love of country and a united "togetherness." After years of unemployment and poverty, the frustrated American working class was more than ready to roll up their sleeves and get to work. Change in every facet of American life was taking place almost overnight. An interesting example of this change occurred in my hometown, St. Paul, Minnesota, when the popular German House Ballroom, located just south of the State Capitol, was renamed the American House Ballroom ... for obvious reasons?

Almost overnight this war began to change America in so many ways. Traditional housewives, whose homemaker occupation had been pretty well written in stone, began entering the work force in large numbers doing various jobs in the war effort and, to everyone's surprise, were even entering the armed forces. When the war ended in 1945, many of these women opted to continue working out of the home. The women's "revolution" from their traditional occupation of homemaking to the world of competitive employment was going full blast. We can thank this war for opening up the employment world to women. This brought more income into the family unit and played a major role in strengthening the economy.

Many African Americans, for years restricted in their selection of occupations, saw the job market open up in a variety of new fields as a result of the expanded war effort. Jim Griffin, Saint Paul's first black chief of police, stated that as a young man in the late 1930s he was fortunate to secure a job with the railroad as a porter. He considered this a prime job for a man of his race at the time. He joined the navy when the war began. In 1945 upon discharge, Jim discovered he was eligible for GI Bill benefits that opened the door to new vocational training and employment opportunities. As a result of veterans preference, he was able to apply and be selected as one of Saint Paul's first black policemen. He also described changes he experienced as a black sailor in the service. When he entered the navy, he reported to the Great Lakes Naval Station and was immediately assigned to an all-black navy unit. Midway during the war, however, under direction of President Truman, government regulations were changed, and integration became mandatory for all military services. He saw this as a giant step in the integration movement. At about this same time, Jackie Robinson, a talented black baseball player, opened the door to integration in the sports world, and our changing society began to take shape with increased integration occurring in housing, employment, and all phases of life in America. This transition to a more integrated society played a significant role in expanding America's growing economy. The GI Bill offering free education to discharged servicemen and servicewomen opened the door to mass numbers of individuals entering college and vocational schools. The result was an expanded middle-class growth in technical and professional occupations. As this expanded middle class grew, so did America's economy.

The war effort was a catalyst to a myriad of new appliances, machines, and other devices and inventions that positively affected the economy and opened the door to many new businesses and industries throughout our country—a movement from iceboxes to refrigerators, coal to gas furnaces, hand shift to automatic shifting automobiles, fans to air conditioning, etc. New affordable homes were built in droves; automobiles were popping off the assembly line like flies, and vacationing was suddenly in the price range of most Americans. Florida here we come! My folks got caught up in this revolution and sold their small home in the Midway District and moved into a much newer and larger home overlooking beautiful Como Lake. I was hoping they would purchase a second car for me to drive. Guess you can't have everything!

In just a few short years our country had moved from its worst depression in history to an exciting, changing world that affected all aspects of our lifestyle and led to a bursting economy. America was on a roll! The country moved into an era where work was plentiful, wages were good, and the economy prospered. This prosperity continued unabated in those years following the war. One can't deny that wars are terrible, because they are, but like it or not, World War II was the catalyst that brought our country out of the doldrums of the Depression into a new era of prosperity!

CHAPTER 5

A New Challenge

Interestingly enough, many of us raised during the heart of the Depression were now living a better life but continued to practice those rules of being frugal even when America's economy flourished. I believe that in the back of our mind was always the fear that, who knows, another depression could be right around the corner, and you bet we'll be ready. I honestly believe those frugal tips we learned from our parents are stashed away in our brains, indelibly embedded there forever. On the other hand, with the economy flourishing we wanted our children to have all of life's amenities that we never had during those tough Depression years. We wanted our children to have the latest toys, to live the good life in updated homes with two bathrooms (or more), two cars in the garage, fashionable clothes, new baseball gloves, a boat, etc. Looking back, maybe we goofed up. In defense of our actions, however, we Depression-raised parents stuck to our conservative upbringing: saved, paid our bills promptly, and stayed out of major debt, playing it financially safe. It was more financially comfortable for us conservative folks to watch football on TV instead of paying to attend games, driving a used car instead of a new one, shopping at Penney's instead of Macy's, and eating at restaurants using a two-for-one coupon instead of splurging at Manny's Steak House. At least that was my philosophy. If another depression was going to occur, you can bet I would be ready!

I'm not sure we were so wrong in wanting our kids to have all the things we never had when we were their age. We wanted them to have the good life. Maybe we just missed the boat, and in our desire to be good parents neglected to teach our kids those conservative values that our parents lived by, and we grew up with. My dad's Economics 101 course was apparently dropped from the "School of Hard Knocks" course list. Yes, I know I'm probably overstating the case a bit, but admit it or not, my kids, and I suspect those of my peers, enjoyed a lot more frills in their lives then we experienced. My elder son attended a year of college in England, and his brother owned an MG Midget with a convertible top when he was sixteen. The speedboat we owned, loaded with my gas, was available for waterskiing whenever the urge came or relatives arrived. On the other hand, I continued to drive a secondhand partially rusted VW Beetle, and then graduated to an economical Pinto. I must confess that it was an awfully good feeling being a "good-time" dad!

Okay, so I'm willing to admit that maybe a good share of us old folks probably screwed up by not spending more time teaching our kids those four key financial principles that my folks lived by and taught us. I guess it was more fun teaching them to be big spenders hoping the world would never change again, and that when they left the roost they could be able to continue this "good life." Well, the good life for a good share of folks entering the working world today has come to an abrupt end. Unfortunately, many now find themselves sitting directly behind that proverbial financial eight ball. If you just happen to be one of those folks in financial distress, maybe a suggestion or two from this conservative old man might help get you back in the game. You really have nothing to lose!

CHAPTER 6

What's Ahead

If you are one of the fortunate few who come from a family of millionaires, or is a member of an Indian tribe operating a gambling casino where each member receives a million dollars plus annually, you just may want to switch to a good mystery book or newspaper to read. On the other hand, it might be fun to keep reading and learn how the other half live. This book is primarily directed at that legion of folks who work for a living making a salary that is never quite enough, and to save anything is simply a dream. A recent report from the federal government indicates that the average family income is slightly under $60,000. This book is targeted to this population and those making well under this figure. I'm referring to that large population of working folks who may earn just enough cash to get by but not enough to get ahead. If you're credit card debt is increasing each month, then I suggest you read on.

A growing challenge facing workers today, which was far less a problem in our day, is the increasing exposure to mass advertisement efforts encouraging you to spend your money to purchase every possible product including the kitchen sink—items you absolutely must have and can't live without. It's almost a form of brainwashing, believing you really can't survive without securing that product. There are restaurants on every corner with exciting special food offers, and how can you possibly survive without that four-dollar cup of fancy coffee from Starbuck's each morning. The TV advertisement telling you $10,500 has been taken off the price of this brand-new pickup truck with every whistle imaginable, however, fails to mention that after this price reduction, the list price is still $55,000. It seems as if fifteen minutes of every thirty-minute evening news and sitcom program is flooded with advertisements. We are being bombarded with "things" we must buy that are essential to our very existence. The credit card is the ticket to this immediate gratification. Why wait? My neighbor just bought a brand-new John Deere lawnmower. Gosh, I want one just like it, and I need it right now because my grass is getting long. My credit card will cover the cost. Oh, the interest rate is 22 percent. I want it anyway! If I'm maxed out on my MasterCard credit card, then I'll use my Visa card. What a great solution. My neighbor's son had a college debt he was paying off monthly, but unfortunately his monthly payment failed to cover even the interest. If he didn't do something drastic, his college debt payment would go on forever. You guessed it; my neighbor paid it off! Not many folks I know have the funds to bail their children out of debt. By the way, after this school loan was paid off, his son immediately purchased that $55,000 pickup truck he always wanted, with a hefty monthly loan payment. Some folks just don't get the message! This is why so many young folks are digging a financial pit with no bottom. It's time to stop digging, and start filling in!

In 1968, I built a house for $27,000 and paid $6,000 for my half-acre lot. In 1986, I sold this home for well over $200,000. In 1987, I bought a ten-acre land parcel for $29,000 and in 2011 sold it for just shy of $300,000. Geez, I must be one great businessman! Thanks for the compliment, but the reality is that I simply lived in the right period of time when inflation was rising like one of those hot-air balloons. If, perish the thought, I was going to build or purchase another home, it certainly wouldn't be in the neighborhood of $27,000 but more like $270,000. Fortunately, at the age of eighty-five, I banked the money from the sale of my home and moved into a retirement residence. Just look at the money I stashed away by not building again! Many of us who are in this eighty-plus age bracket really benefited from this rapid inflationary rise. We purchased items when prices were low and sold off when prices were high. We weren't necessarily smart businesspeople but were just plain lucky. Inflation just made us look smart. Today as we sit in our rocking chair drinking our diet Coke, the world has suddenly become very different. A friend's daughter purchased a new home in 2006 for an estimated price of

$225,000. They later wanted to upgrade to a newer home in 2012, and, to their surprise, a downturn in the economy resulted in their home value slipping to an estimated $175,000. To make matters worse, the demand for new homes had become more competitive, so up goes their purchasing price. Inflation certainly hasn't been a friend to these folks. So when my friend's daughter says, "Dad, life isn't fair; you sell your home and made money, and I sell mine and lose money." He has to remind her that life just isn't fair!

The writing on the wall is telling us that a large number of working folks today are facing a very changing and challenging economic situation far different than we faced in the 1930s and later in the 1980s and 1990s. Let me remind you again that pension plans are becoming a thing of the past; social security, which we old folks thrive on, is in danger of being cut out; job security appears to be slipping away; fringe benefits are disappearing, and inflation is up for grabs. All those employee benefits that we enjoyed since World War II ended are beginning to disappear. I guess I knew when to retire! Today many young folks entering the labor market after leaving college or technical training schools have the added problem of being strapped with school loans. Those young people who moved directly into employment after high school generally fall into the lower- and middle-class wage bracket, with many bogged down with debts plus increasing inflation. Survival is the primary goal of these folks with retirement the last thing on their minds!

So let's summarize. In our current world we are experiencing rising inflation, marginal worker wages, disappearing pension plans, possible loss of Social Security, reduced fringe benefits, mass advertisements for products you're told you absolutely must have, credit and debit cards with no lid, and out of sight interest rates, marginal savings, school debts, etc. It doesn't take a Philadelphia lawyer to figure out that a good share of today's young and middle-aged workers are hanging by their financial fingertips with little eventual hope of moving into my rocking chair. Unfortunately, good ol' dad will most likely not be around to help bail them out. Maybe working till you drop dead for these folks is the long-term solution, but that doesn't sound like much fun. Okay, if this is the case, then let's begin to explore some way out of this dilemma. Let's put on our optimist hat. If our generation could make it out of that devastating

Great Depression of the 1930s, then I'm convinced the current working generation can achieve financial stability that has my rocking chair in their future. To achieve this financial security will require you to store in the back of your mind forever those four key guides to survival:

1. Avoid debt.
2. Always save something.
3. Don't give your money away.
4. Be willing to "think out of the box."

These are the same guides that allowed our parents and grandparents to successfully make it through the Great Depression. View these guides as the bible. Add to your bible a willingness to make certain changes in your life, and don't forget to add the word *sacrifice* to your vocabulary. Also hold off on reading those books on how to work with a financial planner or ten key guides to investment planning. A financial planner can't be of much help if you don't have any savings or are already in debt. My suggestion for those folks who spend $19.50 on one of those expensive financial planner books is to return it immediately to the bookstore, take the cash, and place it into your empty savings account. Now you have $19.50 in your savings, hopefully the beginning of a savings account that will grow. This $19.50 may not be much of a nest egg, but it's a start. Hold off on purchasing those financial planner books until you become financially solvent with some cash in your savings account. Remember, ridding yourself of debts and increasing your income level should be your goal to attain financial freedom. Each generation presents different financial challenges, but those four key guides to survival are the same for each generation. Let's take a look at how these key guides might work in today's world.

SECTION 2

Lessons from the Depression

Putting My Dad's Economics 101 Course into Practice

CHAPTER 7

Rule 1: Avoiding Debt

Each June, thousands of graduates are exiting colleges, universities, and vocational schools anxiously ready to enter the working world, in addition to those high school graduates who made the decision to move directly into the labor market. A large percentage of these young people will take on their assigned careers with enthusiasm, but unfortunately many of those leaving advanced educational programs find themselves with an unexpected burden on their back, called a student loan. Those students who attained full scholarships or come from wealthy families are the fortunate ones. The majority of students, however, who began school debt free, will be less fortunate exiting school, with student loans ranging anywhere from a few thousand up to one hundred thousand dollars or more. One graduate expressed it this way: "It's like starting a race with a bag of cement on your back." How different than in my generation. Student loans in the early 1950s were almost unheard of, and even in the mid-1970s when my children graduated and entered the labor market, they left loan free. A comment I heard from a fellow who graduated two years ago had this to say: "I have a job, but just sneak by financially after paying the rent, the car payment, purchase food, buy those personal necessities, and have a beer once in a while." He then added, "To make it worse, that lousy school loan keeps me at the poverty level." I recently read a magazine article where the president of our state university commented on his concern with those ever-rising tuition rates and student loans. He pointed out that most graduates worked hard to keep their loans to a minimum. He expressed a concern, however, about certain graduates leaving school with unusually high loans primarily due to their over-the-top living style. Those are high loans of their own making. I'm not sure anyone can offer a magic solution to eliminating student loans or to reducing the high cost of living present today, because these financial challenges are most likely here to stay. The real $64,000 question, "your challenge," is how does one become financially solvent as quickly as possible by eliminating these burdensome loan costs and reducing those ever-increasing personal living expenses?

In those years I attended the university, it was far easier to keep my school and living expenses to a minimum and graduate debt free. I used some of the tactics learned from those Depression years to keep my expenses to a minimum. I lived at home so avoided any rent or dormitory expense, hitchhiked or took the streetcar to avoid travel expense, carried a bag lunch most of the time, always had a side job, made a few bucks refereeing intramural sports along with some side money playing in a dance band. I graduated debt free and with a few dollars in my pocket. In the 1970s, when two of my kids went off to college and lived on campus, the agreed-upon plan was that I would pay the room and board, and they pay the tuition, which was far less than today. Both children worked during the summers and often during the school year to fully pay their tuition and book expenses. By following this plan, they both were fortunate to graduate debt free. Today, without the help of a "good daddy" or an academic or athletic scholarship, I question if it's even possible to leave college without a school debt. Those young people who avoided college and directly entered the employment world may not be saddled with a school debt, but many still are financially challenged by the existing high cost of living.

I would be the first to admit that it was far easier to graduate debt free and live more economically in my youthful days than it is today. So what is the solution to these financial challenges facing our young workers? First off, studying how similar problems were solved in the past might gain an idea or two, and, second, we need to "think out of the box" for new solutions, and, third, there has to be a willingness to change our ways, which may be the biggest challenge. I love change, but lots of people don't!

Climbing out of the Hole

Having major debts hanging over your head while earning a limited income is like having a millstone around your neck when you go swimming. You can't stay above water, so you're in danger of drowning. My emphatic suggestion is to rid yourself of those debts as quickly as possible so your income can be directed at more positive outcomes. Those interest payments, your millstone, if allowed to drag on and on will keep you at the bottom of the pool just struggling for air. My dad held to this rule: "Never buy anything till you pay off your debts. That loan interest is wasted money. Get rid of your loans as fast as you can." This advice from a man who made it through the Depression sounds old-fashioned, but in today's world I would agree with my dad in suggesting you rid yourself of those "unproductive loans" as quickly as possible. An unproductive loan falls into the school loan category because this loan has already served its purpose; it is past tense, and it offers nothing "concrete" for you now. A "productive loan" would fall into the category of a home mortgage, an automobile, a washing machine, etc.—something very tangible that benefits you in the future. My suggestion is to follow my dad's recommendation and pay off those nonproductive loans as quickly as possible so you are in a better financial position to take on those productive loans that will enhance your future. That nonproductive interest is truly your millstone to a more productive future. I asked the son of a good friend who had graduated some five years ago if he had a school loan. He said, "I sure did but decided to hold off on making any long-term financial plans until this loan was paid off in full. I cut my living expenses to an absolute minimum and had that school debt paid off in just three years." This fellow was willing to sacrifice for those three years to gain his financial freedom. That's something to think about!

I heartily endorse this young man's plan and recommend to each person burdened with a school loan or any other nonproductive loan to set aside a three- to five-year time period to rid yourself of that debt, your millstone. The primary objective of this three- to five-year period will require two specific tasks: (1) reduce your living expenses to the minimum, and (2) maximize your income. Now for you folks who need immediate gratification, who want to live the good life right from the start, this will be a true challenge. That word *sacrifice* was the necessary word of the day in those years of the Great Depression. I suggest you also adopt *sacrifice* as your word of the day to rid yourself of that debt, the millstone strapped to your back. Put blinders on to avoid all those distractions and temptations that will detour you from this goal. Those folks who survived the Depression had to put blinders on to avoid going into debt, and so should you. Remember, to sacrifice early will lead to financial freedom later. Purchasing that brand new $60,000 truck might just have to wait. Visit the used car lot!

Reduce Residence Expenses

After leaving the university, I briefly remained living in my parents' home to save a buck. Today a number of young people have followed this plan after finding out the hard way that apartment living can be expensive and can quickly drain the budget. For the majority of young people, however, this may not be a possibility, so finding a reasonably priced place to live becomes a number one priority. Recently a young lady told me, "I found a nice apartment, but the rent is high and continues to increase, so I may be forced to move. Rent costs are expensive all over this town, so I'm not sure what to do." Nearly everyone has their eye on those apartments with all the frills. Let's look at some other less expensive living possibilities. Remember what Mr. Enter and Mr. Lennon did to save rent during the Depression. They rented a room in our home. They saved money by this move, and on the other hand my folks made a buck ... not a bad plan for both parties. We are living in a time when renting a room or two in private homes is becoming more popular. In the 1980s after our children left home, we decided to rent one of our vacant bedrooms to a young lady who had just secured a teaching job in our town. With her low entry-level salary, she was trying to save money to pay off her school loan and put enough money away to eventually have her own apartment. She realized that renting a room in a private home was far cheaper than the cost of moving into one of the local apartment buildings. Now if sharing the bath is foreign to you, just remember that in the 1930s most every farm family had that fancy outdoor toilet that everyone had to share. My brother and I shared our one bathroom with my folks and a renter during the Depression, and we survived; you will survive as well. Renting a room in a private home requiring you to share the bathroom is well worth the sacrifice that in time will lead to that fancy apartment with all the amenities or owning your own home when that unproductive loan is paid off. Remember, to sacrifice early will lead to gratification later!

Let me share another interesting thought to consider when looking for an inexpensive residence. More and more elderly folks living in large homes have spare rooms that could easily be made available for renters. As these folks age, they might well benefit by having a roomer to assist them with certain home chores. This extra help may also lead to an even lower rent. I've heard of some older folks wanting to remain in their home who actually offered free rent for someone to help with necessary home tasks. Many of these elderly folks may never have considered renting a room and recognizing its potential benefits. If this type living arrangement appeals to you, then be aggressive in locating such residences ... wow, a chance to "think out of the box." You may find that home nursing companies may be an excellent resource for identifying those prospective homes that would benefit from your presence. This type of housing arrangement offers a twofold benefit; lower living costs for you with money available to attack your school loan, plus a possible service benefit for elderly folks. Your goal is to save a buck, but helping others offers another plus!

Another interesting approach to saving rent money is to pair up with a good friend or friends in a living setting that would reduce rent expenses to half or to a third. I understand this to be an excellent plan if your roommate(s) and you are compatible. When my son got married, his wife already was renting a home. They thought it would save them the cost of their rent and taxes if they allowed two of their good friends to reside in two of the vacant bedrooms. All went well for a while until my son found food missing and the two renters slowly taking over their living room. In time, all the house rules fell apart; that's if they had rules in the first place. Needless to say, these fellows were told to leave, and their friendships went with them. So if this approach to saving rent money is your plan, make sure that you are compatible with each other and that house rules are written in stone. This living arrangement can work if you properly prepare for it and realize that your rule book may not be the same rule book others follow.

My wife and I had kind of a unique experience in finding a residence when we arrived home from our honeymoon in 1952. I learned of a newspaper man who was going on a six-month sabbatical and wanted to rent his fully furnished apartment during that time period. We grabbed it and immediately paid our first month's rent of fifty dollars. The apartment was fully furnished and located in one of Saint Paul's upscale neighborhoods with stores and shops of all varieties in easy walking distance. The apartment even included a music room with a piano. I always had the desire to play the piano so immediately signed up to take Charlie Johnson's quick learning piano course, hoping I could bang out a few tunes before our six-month residence ended. I learned the hard way that it takes more than six months to learn to play the piano. That was one hundred dollars blown right down the drain. I should have sued Charlie Johnson for false advertising! Well, for every "hiccup" in life, there generally is something good that occurs. The good was that fifty dollars a month rent.

Our six-month extravagant living experience ended very quickly, and reality set in. Our limited income led us to an older home on Hague Avenue in Saint Paul with a converted apartment on the second floor. The landlord lived on the first floor, and we shared the second floor with a kind old lady who was very nice but spent way too much time in the bathroom we shared with her. We entered this apartment through the bedroom, which was kind of unique. The rent was cheap; we were in love, and, frankly, at that early stage of our married life who cared? Anyway, this apartment living was really cheap, and we knew in time our dream home was just waiting for us. Our best friend had one of those attractive apartments with all the amenities, but it was three times as expensive as our apartment. We were saving money for an eventual home of our own. My friend's goal was apparently different. He wanted immediate gratification, but we were looking toward the future!

In 1989, after living in ten different homes, my wife and I built our final dream home in a beautiful country setting and lived there for twenty-four wonderful years. I remembered the financial benefits my folks gained by renting one of their bedrooms during those Depression years so decided I would give the rental business a try as well. I converted my lower level into a complete apartment with a full kitchen, two bathrooms, living room and fireplace, plus a private patio entrance and garage. It turned out to be an easy moneymaker, and the renters ended up being good friends. Years later I put an addition on our home that included a complete mother-in-law apartment with all the amenities including a fireplace plus a private entrance, patio, and garage. These two rentals offered substantial extra income for us, but my two renters benefited even more because they loved the country environment and low rental rate. I charged each renter a reasonable rate of $800 a month with absolutely no additional costs. Each renter agreed that a similar rental in other local apartment buildings would far exceed our monthly rental rate. The toughest task I faced when we decided to sell this home and move into our current retirement residence was to inform my two renters that they would have to move. Needless to say, they were quite unhappy to move back to the real world and higher-priced rentals. If, like my folks, I had offered them simply a bedroom to rent, their monthly rate would even have been lower. These two renters were looking for an inexpensive living setting just like so many young folks today entering the labor market for the first time. I simply wanted to cover our home mortgage expense. There are many living arrangements in our community very suitable for renting that may not even be listed on the rental market. My mother didn't ask that hobo to come to our house for a free meal; he was innovative enough to figure out a means to get a free meal. It's really up to you to be innovative as well and seek out rental opportunities that may not even be listed. Take a lesson from the hobo and convince someone that he or she has a great rental possibility that will make him or her some extra money. Be willing to "think out of the box." You can't be bashful in today's world!

Searching for the least expensive type living arrangement is one of the smartest approaches to saving money to pay off debts and to begin a savings plan. Living conservatively, especially in those first three to five years of your working career, may be a sacrifice, but, believe me, it will pay dividends for you in the future.

Reducing Daily Living Expenses

Now let's be honest, are you one of those individuals that purchases your groceries, clothing, and all other needs at whatever store is convenient with no concern for price? Have you ever uttered these words: "I just don't have the time or patience to shop around, looking for sales or better deals; it's just not my thing!" I'd like to introduce people with this attitude to my wife, who was raised in the Depression, who says, "Shopping for the best deal and lowest price is like a game; it's fun, takes very little time, and it pays off." It's the way she saves us a bundle of money each month. It's just another reminder that saving money is what this book is all about. A fellow commented the other day, "If I spot a nickel on the ground, I don't bother to even pick it up. What can a nickel buy in today's inflated economy?" What he fails to realize is that a nickel here and another nickel there will add up, and pretty soon you have a dollar. A dollar will buy a tube of toothpaste at the Dollar Store, but in a Walgreens drugstore that tooth paste will cost $1.75 or more, and that seventy-five-cents savings will buy one White Castle hamburger with a few cents left over. So, the premise is simple. If you are serious about saving money, then go for the sales, the bargains, the freebies, the deals! Listen to what the expert, my wife, has to say: "By playing the savings game, I can easily stay within our monthly budget, and it's surprising just how much I can stash away." Believe me, exceeding the monthly budget in our family is a definite no-no. If you are truly interested in saving a buck in your day-to-day life, then listen carefully to my wife's tactics. By the way, age has sharpened her mind. Listed below are some of her thoughts and techniques on buying smart at a reduced price. Keep in mind that this is all about ridding yourself of debts and saving money.

Food and Personal Items

1. If the grocery store you frequent has a clerk that bags groceries, then more than likely your groceries will cost more. That clerk has to be paid.
2. Shopping at "discount" grocery stores will offer lower prices. They generally offer more off-brand products and have a plain store decor, and you always bag your own groceries.
3. Check sale tables in most stores. They generally offer some good deals, but be cautious and check expiration dates.
4. Many grocery type stores and bakeries have a section for day-old bakery goods. Microwave ovens are wonderful!

5. Weekly newspaper ads or flyers for varied stores will list sale items or offer discount coupons. Cut them out and keep them in your car. Yes, men can also use them!

6. Some grocery stores set aside a day a week as a "special" day, offering 5 percent or 10 percent off on all purchases. Wednesday is the "special" day at one of our local grocery stores.

7. Certain stores offer check-out cards for shoppers. Each time you shop at their store, they check off that day, and when the card is full, you get a reward—a free turkey for Thanksgiving, a free bag of groceries, etc.

8. Large box stores may offer more sale items, cheaper products, or larger purchase orders than the smaller stores. That's great for families that have adequate storage or freezer room. Oh, yes, they also offer food testing stations. If you're hungry, these testing stations may just satisfy your lunch appetite. Be careful about overbuying items that may sit never used in your cupboard.

9. Always make out a shopping list prior to grocery shopping and stick to it. This will avoid purchasing items you may not need. Note: for men, this is an absolute must!

10. Don't shop when you are hungry. Those bakery goods you don't need will end up in your shopping cart.

11. Avoid the premium steak section in the meat department; you will end up in the poorhouse.

Clothing and Incidentals

1. Generally stores with readily available clerks to wait on you will have higher prices. The Kohl's, Penney's type stores where you select and try on products on your own and carry them to the cashier will be cheaper. Check out those stores offering never-ending sales and discounts. Someday I honestly believe Kohl's will pay us to shop at their store.

2. Stores such as Goodwill and consignment stores offer a wide assortment of clothing, jewelry, and other miscellaneous items at very reasonable prices. Carefully selected secondhand clothing will save a bundle.

3. The true "dollar" type store offers a full assortment of food, personal, and family needs for the low price of one dollar. Visit one of these stores, and you will marvel at your savings. Buy two birthday cards for one dollar at the dollar store, then compare that to the price of a single birthday card at your local drugstore. Need I say more?

4. Estate, garage, and newspaper want ad sales are sources of clothing and family and personal items, generally at a far reduced cost than purchased at a retail store. Check out what your neighbors are almost giving away.

5. The computer has opened the door to purchasing an unlimited array of products of all sorts without leaving the house. Immediate delivery and free shipping are common practices. Amazon is one of the most popular of these companies, but other companies offering computer buying are currently flooding the market. I should point out that companies such as Amazon and those other computer-generated companies are new on the block and offer fairly low prices for just about anything you want to purchase. This has presented a real challenge for the more traditional walk-in retail stores in our community. To counteract this new competition, many of the traditional stores have agreed to match their prices to keep customers happy and to get them to continue shopping in their stores. Whichever direction you wish to go in your shopping practice, keep in mind that price is the important issue, and saving a buck is your goal; write that in stone.

6. Boutique and private entrepreneur sales are prevalent throughout the community. These sales are held in private homes, churches, local shops, and in local town markets. Products for sale are usually locally produced by the seller or purchased for sale from specialty companies and are generally reasonably priced. Shopping in some of these nontraditional settings can offer some unusually good bargains plus an opportunity to locate some items on your "to buy" list.

Not long ago my wife and I had a few minutes of free time before meeting with our physician. We were just a block away from the

Lutheran thrift store and decided to stop in. In those few minutes, I purchased a special baseball hat for three dollars that sold at the sports store in our shopping mall for thirty-two dollars. My wife located, on one the clothing racks, a name brand jacket that had a sale price of $5.00, but on this particular day everything was half price, so that coat cost her $2.50. The cost of this jacket at the local department store was $45.50. My daughter-in-law buys all her clothes at either Goodwill or other selected discount type stores and, by the way, has the reputation of being very well-dressed. Remember the old saying that "someone's junk can be your treasure." It's just another reminder that saving money is your goal!

Entertainment

If you regularly attend the theater, professional sporting events, concerts, and other events that cost anywhere from thirty-five dollars to one hundred dollars to attend, your goal to reduce your debt and begin a savings program is on the road to disaster. I suggest you put these events on your back burner until you are financially solvent. On the other hand, don't be bashful in contacting friends who may have free tickets, and be sure to check on available performances or events with reduced matinee and group prices that won't cost you an arm or a leg. Watching these events on TV or in a bar while drinking your favorite beverage may not be as exciting as actually attending but is certainly less expensive. Having friends over for a TV viewing party with beer and chips is certainly a far less expensive substitute. Let me remind you that high school, college, and amateur sporting, musical, and theater events are reasonably priced and offer excellent entertainment value. They are also a great way to help support the activities in your local community.

Many health insurance plans now cover the cost of members to attend local health clubs. This is not only beneficial to your personal health but offers an excellent social outlet for meeting new friends as well. If your insurance plan doesn't cover this cost, check out the YMCA or other less expensive exercise programs that are affordable. I also urge you to check out all the free and low-cost entertainment opportunities in your community. For example, the city of Saint Paul has beautiful Como Park and zoo, the Winter Carnival, the Saint Paul Saints baseball team, Harriet Island, numerous bike trails, and unlimited other recreational opportunities. Remember, the folks living through that Great Depression had little if any money to spend on entertainment. They had to find ways for having fun by attending social activities and events that were free because they had no money. Your challenge is the same as theirs. I hope you are up for the challenge!

Restaurants and Eating Out

In those challenging 1930s, most every working-class family ate their meals sitting around the kitchen or dining room table at home. My senior friends and a good share of the elderly residents living in my retirement residence are unanimous in stating that none of them ate in restaurants in their early years because it was simply too expensive. To put it bluntly, eating out in those Depression years was a luxury no one could afford. I guess I was the fortunate one to sneak in a few White Castle hamburgers when I could talk my dad out of a dime. If you are committed to climbing out of debt, then eating in restaurants on a regular basis is a luxury you simply can't afford. If you are aware of selected restaurants where costs are similar to the cost of eating at home, then go for it. It makes sense to reward yourself by eating out in one of those nice restaurants just once or twice a month. Do you really need that expensive cup of exotic coffee each morning at Starbucks? Here are a few guides to follow when it comes to eating out:

1. When folks ask what gift you want for your birthday or other key holidays, put a restaurant card as your number one suggestion.
2. Always check the menu and particularly that right side (the price) before ordering. That T-bone steak may be tasty for $24.00, but the $8.50 hamburger steak with mushrooms will fill you up just as much.
3. Some restaurants offer "specials" on certain slow customer days. A restaurant in our local community offers a two-for-one deal on Sundays and Mondays.
4. Certain restaurants offer a regular menu plus a lower cost dinner 'special' for each day of the week. There are also those

    restaurants that offer menu items with smaller portions ... for diet conscious folks.

5.   Breakfast and lunch menus at most restaurants are at a much-reduced price than the evening dinner menu.

6.   Many restaurants advertise "specials" in local newspapers or community flyers: all you can eat Friday fish fry for $8.50, a prime rib special dinner every Tuesday for $12.00, a one-topping pizza on Thursday for $9.00.

7.   Purchasing prepared, uncooked food to take home and cook yourself is cheaper than most restaurant food. For example, pizza all prepared for you to cook at home offers a real savings versus the cost for a similar pizza in a restaurant.

8.   Cafeteria eating establishments offer a greater variety of food offerings, and an unlimited quantity of food at your disposal for a reasonable price, and that's good for family dining.

9.   Food at sporting and other professional sponsored events are always more expensive. Enjoy the event and eat at a local restaurant before or after the event for far less cost, or, better yet, eat at home before or after you attend the event.

10. Many churches, American Legion, VFW clubs, and related organizations offer special steak fries, fish dinners, spaghetti suppers, and hamburger nights as money-raising events. They are always reasonably priced.

11. Many folks have adopted the practice of purchasing one meal on a menu and sharing that meal with their partner. This is the way to cut your dinner price in half.

12. Check out the food menus in your local bars. Many offer "specials" at a very reasonable price, and, believe me, hamburgers from bars are the best. A local bar/restaurant offers a $3.75 hamburger and another bar/restaurant has a complete dinner special for $8.50.

13. If it's your thing, then fast-food restaurants are usually reasonably priced and are on most street corners. They all seem to offer, at times, very inexpensive specials. White Castle and Culver's are my favorite.

14. Find a boyfriend or girlfriend that is willing to pay the full dinner bill. Pick your dates carefully!

I recall in my dating years taking my girlfriend to the White Castle restaurant pretty often and to a French restaurant on Selby Avenue in Saint Paul that served cinnamon toast and a fruit dish that cost just one dollar. When I really wanted to impress my date, I took her to the Roman Cafe in downtown Saint Paul that offered a bacon-wrapped steak dinner special for two dollars, and that two dollars pretty well emptied my billfold. Keeping out of debt was my primary goal, as it should be yours. When my wife and I were first married, one of our regular meals was a Spam dinner that she prepared to taste just like ham. Our big night out during those first couple of years of marriage actually consisted of staying home on a Saturday night, grilling one of those inexpensive steaks but with all the trimmings, and watching an uninterrupted movie on TV. We seldom, if ever, ate out at restaurants. I shouldn't have to explain why. Keeping out of debt and saving a few dollars was my primary goal. Ridding yourself of those nonproductive debts should be your goal as well.

Transportation

While hitchhiking offered a wonderful means of free transportation in those Depression years, I recommend you scratch it off your list. I'm afraid if you tried this technique today you most likely would be arrested on the spot, end up in jail, and be fined. This technique worked in my day, but, trust me, it won't work for you in today's world. It seems everyone I know owns at least one car, and a good share of folks own two or more. Check the freeways at four thirty in the afternoon, and, while sitting dead in the traffic, you'd swear that everyone owns five or six cars. You might be able to sneak by without owning a car in New York City with cabs so plentiful, but in mid-America with sprawling suburbs and cities so spread out, owning a car appears almost a necessity. Here's a warning, please be careful, and don't fall for all those advertisements regarding new and used car sales. You know, those enticing ads pleading with you to purchase today, or during fair week because of their amazing discounted prices, or if you purchase that new car from our dealership there will be no payment for six months. Our sale price on that new truck is reduced today by $10,000 but fail to tell you the price is still $55,000, or the monthly payment is $450 or more. If you believe these wonderful claims, you may find yourself heading into a major financial pit that's hard to crawl out of. I've fallen into that pit more than once in my lifetime and learned a few things the hard way.

Let's be honest, most of us are enamored with the idea of owning a brand-new car. I had my eye on that brand new slick-looking VW yellow convertible back in 1960. It was my dream car, but it took every bit of my savings plus a generous car loan. In fact, I didn't have enough available cash to purchase the car radio. I really loved the car, but those car payments were bleeding me dry along with the discovery that the insurance and annual license fees were higher for new cars than for used cars. A fellow I befriended on one of our church committees owned a local used car lot. I figured a guy that goes to church must have some honesty in him, and fortunately I found that to be true. I ended up purchasing nearly all my cars from his used car lot in future years. My used car payments were lower, his costs for repair were far less than in the new car dealerships, and, most of all, I could trust his honesty about the cars I purchased. I was able to put the glamour of owning a brand-new car aside and realized the financial benefits of purchasing used cars from an honest and reputable used car dealer. Search around and ask your friends their opinion on honest car dealerships. If you don't already know, there are people in this world that you can't trust! By the way, now that I'm retired, I only drive brand new cars; the wait was worth it!

My granddaughter lives in the suburbs and works in the city. To save on gas, parking fees, and freeway hassles, she drives her car to the local train or bus station and then uses the train or bus to get to and from work. In addition to the financial savings, she arrives home with a smile on her face. Some folks ride share together, substantially reducing their transportation expenses. The current trend for folks to work from their homes is even a better way of saving on transportation expenses, because there are none! There are two additional suggestions to be considered as a savings for all drivers. Gas is an expensive item that can be reduced if you use those five-, seven-, or ten-cents-per-gallon discounts offered at a number of gas stations. Why pay the full gas price if you can pay at a reduced rate? When you purchase groceries at our local grocery store and then purchase gas at its station, the savings they offer is even better, up to twenty cents a gallon. By the way, you can save on auto insurance rates by using the many different discounts. I purchase my auto insurance from a company that deals with sixteen different insurance companies. This allows me to compare rates between companies and to secure the best discount offer. You should also know there is a substantial savings on your auto insurance policy if you pay annually rather than monthly. Certain insurance companies also offer towing services as part the insurance plan, saving you the traditional cost of purchasing towing service as a separate entity. Other insurance discounts reward good driving habits. Don't be bashful about asking for them.

Saving Together

If paying your debt off and saving money is your primary goal as you begin your work career, and you meet that special girl or fellow, your life equation changes. Once the fateful question is asked and the response is yes, a new factor enters the picture because now there are two people who must share this goal. This can lead to a wonderful partnership, or it's possible the two of you may have divergent life goals. Check out the movie *The Odd Couple*, where partners see life differently, and the entanglements can create complications. This movie was a comedy but in real life can lead to tragedy.

Before any marriage commitments, I suggest you spend an evening or two discussing your goals in life. It may be too late for this discussion after the marriage! One of my high school classmates really lucked out. He met this society gal on a vacation trip and fell madly in love. It just happened that her dad was president of a large and very successful manufacturing company. When marriage was eminent, her dad offered him a job in the company with unlimited potential for the future. This might have been the best way for the father to keep an eye on his new son-in-law. I know this friend pretty well, and, believe me, the father knew exactly what he was doing. In any event, he was one of those guys at the right place at the right time. What a friend he turned out to be; not once did he invite my wife and me for dinner at his fancy country club. I've since taken him off my good buddy list. To spend time sharing his goals in life with the new wife would probably be just a waste of time. If this friend ends up getting a divorce, this book should be required reading. Frankly, society gals never interested me. My goal was to marry the best-looking gal in town.

A friend, over a beer, told me about their beautiful wedding and that exciting weeklong honeymoon in downtown Chicago. He said they returned home still madly in love. A few days after returning home, his new wife had lunch with a girlfriend who told her about a townhouse that just came on the market in her old neighborhood. She was all excited and said it would be the perfect place for them to start their life together. They checked it out, and it had everything they wanted: two bedrooms, a fireplace, washer and dryer, heated garage, and access to a great party room. Oh, yes, there was one problem. The price was $1,800 a month. This place would have devoured most of their entire monthly income. She gently squeezed my friend's hand, and said ever so sweetly, "But, honey, I just love it." He tells me, "I had a problem." I told him, "No, you had an opportunity."

The first thought that came to his mind was, "We simply can't afford it," and added, "My dad left that chapter out of his marriage orientation course." I asked how he handled it, and he said, "Well, I gave her a passionate kiss, then said, 'Honey, it's just way to expensive,' and held my breath." She wasn't happy, but after some explanation and a few more hugs and kisses, she agreed that it was awfully expensive. Two weeks later, they moved into a small but cute one-bedroom apartment over the neighborhood grocery store. The rent was $795 a month, way, way below the rent in that classy apartment. This friend deserves a medal for good frugal planning and being a skillful politician, and he did it without the help of his dad's advice. I learned over the years that dads aren't always right. There are times in an emergency when we simply have to begin making our own decisions. What a smart way for this couple to begin their marriage. The apartment they moved into was decent but not fancy. It was well within their price range, and they avoided falling into an early financial hole and allowed themselves to save considerable money. This reminds me of an unwritten rule coaches follow when applying for a job. "Avoid following a winning coach; it's better to follow a losing coach. There is only one way to go, and that is up." In a way, this couple decided to also follow this rule by beginning their marriage in a decent but lower-rent residence. It was the first stepping stone in their climb leading hopefully to their eventual dream home. A major pitfall for young folks entering the labor market is to start their lives in an expensive setting with all the amenities only to discover their climb out of debt, or to their eventual dream home, is laden with financial obstacles almost impossible to overcome. Just think, this couple saved $1,005 a month to help pay off their debts and to start saving for the future. It's like being in a marathon race: start slow, pace yourself, and then give it all you've got as you near the finish line! There's usually a way to reduce your residence expense, if you are willing to sacrifice and think of the future rather than just the present.

I also lucked out and did find the best-looking gal in town. She came from a family loaded with love but slightly weak on the finances. I learned quickly that both of us having been born and raised in those Depression years shared a conservative approach to life. I really lucked out! Let me tell you how it all began. After graduating from high school, I was fortunate to secure a job, as the paid pitcher for the town baseball team in New Prague, Minnesota. My weekly salary averaged $120 a week plus access to a small apartment above one of the local eateries. This income also included working at the golf club during the week. It was starvation wages but enough to get by … but not enough to purchase a car or live it up with style. Hitchhiking was my best and cheapest ticket to transportation in those days, when my dad's car wasn't available to borrow. So, in addition to keeping my pitching arm in shape for two baseball games a week, I also spent time exercising my thumb, the same required tool needed during those Depression years to secure free transportation. I quickly learned after a few weeks that this small rural town had a great dance hall known for its exciting old-time polka dances. I had played the tuba in the Sauerkraut's polka band in high school, so polka music was sort of in my blood. I was looking for a little excitement, and this dance hall was right up my alley. Now I needed a date. Dancing alone isn't much fun. I called the accordion player from the Sauerkraut's polka band, who lived in Saint Paul, and told him to get a date and drive that sixty miles the next Sunday to cheer me on at the ball game in the afternoon and to dance the night away to that exciting polka music. He agreed and then asked the name of my date. I told him I wasn't sure, but that I'd find one. I called about eight gals from Saint Paul that I knew, but all were busy (at least that's what they told me). Now what to do? In desperation, I finally remembered this cute gal in our high school class named Toodie, who I heard had recently broken up with her boyfriend (the quarterback on our high school football team). When I called her, she hesitated for a moment and thought she remembered me. To make matters worse she said, "You're taking me dancing, where?" I said, "At the beautiful Park Ballroom in New Prague." She said, "I never heard of it, but, okay, I guess I'll go." She had already committed to our date, so when I broke the news that my friend would pick her up, because I was living that summer in New Prague, she was almost forced to agree with this unusual absentee arrangement. Wow, I should go into sales! I pitched the local team to a victory that Sunday afternoon and danced the night away with this beautiful gal who was as graceful as a feather and never missed a beat. Little did I know she had been a tap dancer. I may have missed a beat or two, but she didn't seem to mind. This was the beginning of a four-year courtship that has led to sixty-six years of marriage bliss. Let me tell you, I won twice that Sunday in July of 1948!

Remember, setting goals in starting your adult life is very important. This gal had goals that seemed to match mine perfectly. No way was I going to let this gal escape from being my wife.

Toodie had a million positive assets in her favor, but unfortunately for me her dad was not the president of the Minnesota Coke plant where he worked and in fact wasn't even the general manager, so, if you haven't guessed, there was no executive job waiting for me after our marriage. As a matter of fact, her dad, who was a wonderful man, worked as a foreman on the coke plant ovens. This was one of those jobs where you wear wooden shoes to avoid the blazing heat of the ovens and required a shower each day after work to remove the coal dust. His wages were meager, so they couldn't afford a car. In fact, when Toodie was a sophomore in high school, her dad had a heart attack that put the family in financial distress. To help out with finances, she went to work after school and on weekends alongside her mother in the heat of a local dry cleaning establishment. In short, her family was rich in so many ways but not when it came to cash. She worked most of her high school years to purchase her own personal needs and to contribute to their family income. She was never available to try out for the cheerleading team, to be a homecoming queen candidate, or to join most other school organizations because of her work schedule. She would have been the prettiest queen Wilson High School ever had. Let's face it, if I was looking for a gal to fall in love with who could enhance my future financial life, I was barking up the wrong tree. I probably should have checked out her family credentials before dating her. On the other hand, she knew what it meant to sacrifice, to work hard, and to achieve something meaningful in this world. Our goals in life matched perfectly. There would be no *Odd Couple* problems in this family!

The partnership we had together was truly a match made in heaven. Our four-year courtship is a wonderful example of how easy it is to sneak by on meager funds when you and your partner are on the same wavelength. We both knew that saving money for our future was our goal. I borrowed my dad's car for most dates, which consisted chiefly of car rides, attending a movie, splurging for a malt at Bridgman's Ice Cream Parlor, or having dinner at the White Castle restaurant. Another fun date was visiting my grandparents for an exciting game of euchre and topping it off with a dish of ice cream. I also began my sports officiating career during my courting days and had the good fortune of officiating the preliminary games played prior to the Minneapolis Lakers professional basketball games at the Minneapolis Auditorium. Not only was this a free date with Toodie, but I was paid the sum total of two dollars a game. To top it off we were given front-row seats right on the edge of the basketball court. In a way, we were celebrities! Who said you couldn't have fun and still save money? Toodie never complained about my being cheap (I mean frugal). I hesitate to imagine just how long our courtship would have lasted if she had come from one of those families that lived the lifestyle of the rich and wealthy. Too many dinners at the White Castle restaurant would have most likely put an abrupt end to our relationship. Fortunately, Toodie seemed to like those White Castle hamburgers as much as I did.

Once I popped the "let's get married" question, I knew there were some big decisions to be made, mostly financial. My dad was my role model when it came to financial issues, so in purchasing that key engagement ring, I planned to put his bartering skills into practice. I found myself in a real dilemma. I was faced with the decision of purchasing a fancy, very large, diamond ring at a discount jewelry store, and the price was right. On the other hand, there was this high-class jewelry store where all the Saint Paul elite shopped on Sixth Street in downtown Saint Paul. Believe me, this was the classiest jewelry store in town without question. The diamond ring they showed me was in my price range, but you really needed 20-20 vision to see the diamond. It was this fancy jewelry store, however, which really impressed me, and I thought would impress Toodie. I said to myself, *What would my dad do in this situation?* I knew he would have gone to the fancy jewelry store and offered them a reduced price. You know, let's negotiate! So, I tried that tactic with absolutely no success. (Apparently I didn't observe my dad's bartering skills close enough). Well, the long and short of it was that the fancy jewelry store salesman won out, and I reluctantly weakened and paid the full $150 price, which was a ton of money in those days. I never told my dad what I paid; he might have disowned me. I should add that this ring did come with a fancy gift box that I felt would impress Toodie. The box was perfect, but it was the size of the diamond that had me somewhat concerned. I considered including a magnifying glass with the ring but thought it might be in bad taste. Toodie seemed to really love the fancy box and did smile when she saw the ring; she has great tact! I do remember that she did ask if that beautiful setting contained a diamond. I told her that the diamond was rather small but was of the highest quality and very petite, just like her. I also reminded her that quality is better than quantity!

We had a wonderful marriage ceremony with all the trimmings and did it on a shoestring. There was no fee for the church service; Toodie's folks held the wedding lunch at their home; the wedding dance was held in the evening at the 3M Hall paid for by my parents. Her folks paid for the supper at the dance. The band played for free because it was their gift to me as a band member, and the dollar dance raised enough cash to pay for our honeymoon. So, you see, from the very beginning of our marriage we were setting the tone for an enjoyable but frugal lifestyle. My dad was proud of my planning and told me, "I was a chip off the old block." (I never told him about the ring fiasco.) We had begun our new married life in a conservative manner but didn't miss out on having a wonderful wedding at a far reduced cost than most of my friends. This save a buck lifestyle, following the lessons learned from living through those Depression years, continued into the future, allowing us to enjoy everything we would need in life but at a reasonable cost. I guess I needed just a bit more training in negotiating skills!

My point is simple; pick the right gal to spend your life with. This is vitally important. Marriage is truly a partnership, and you want to make sure you and your partner are on the same wavelength when it comes to setting and achieving both your short- and long-term financial goals. Be careful and don't fall head over heels in love with a gal who has her eyes on the fancy country club scene. It may work out, but the odds are probably not in your favor. Before you make any marriage commitments, scope out the ballpark. Get to know the family and how they live. If it's all fine clothes from Macy's, classy cars, luxury homes, and regular dates at dad's country club, logic says that you most likely will be expected to continue this lifestyle. A word to the wise says get to know your girlfriend's mother because most likely she will in time end up being much like her. I'm not sure about the father. Here is a simple tip; when you visit with your girlfriend's mother, does she offer you cocktails or a can of diet coke? This may be the clue as to whether you decide to stay or run like hell!

What in the world does my courtship and marriage plans have to do with your future financial life? The answer is lots! How you and your partner begin your life together really sets the tone for your future right to the moment you reach those golden years. Toodie and I, both raised in that conservative Depression period, began from the very beginning working off the same song sheet, living a conservative lifestyle to achieve enough savings to purchase our own home, have a family, and live an enjoyable life. Not a fancy life but a wonderful life! We began our courtship in this conservative manner, got married in a conservative manner, and never strayed from living conservatively the remainder of our lives, and, interestingly enough, we achieved our goals and did just about everything all other married couples did and probably more. From the very beginning we recognized that I most likely was never going to be a millionaire, so by living this conservative lifestyle our plan was to begin "thinking out of the box" in ways that would allow us to live a full and enjoyable life that would eventually lead to those comfortable retirement rocking chairs. Someday our rocking chair can be yours if you are willing to do a little sacrificing, rid yourself of those nasty debts early in your career, and work toward building a savings account to achieve those items in life you both want.

Earlier in the book I shared the story of my friend's father who, during the heart of the Depression, couldn't sell the vegetables from his truck garden and in desperation tried a new sales approach. He traveled in his old pickup truck to Duluth, Minnesota, to sell his vegetables to the cooks on those Lake Superior oar boats. He put everything else in his life aside to travel that long grueling journey twice a day. His willingness to sacrifice in those early days to start this new business paid off and led eventually to a very successful nationwide business in the years that followed. I'll say it again, "Sacrifice early, and enjoy the benefits later." Don't let those unproductive debts linger beyond that three- to five-year period. Get rid of that millstone as quickly as possible and move on to more productive efforts.

CHAPTER 8

Rule 2: Build a Savings Account

A Work History
More work experience equals more work potential.

The Depression offered the best on the job training (OJT) program for teaching folks how to survive in that dormant economy of the 1930s. This OJT program, I call it the Art Schultz Economics 101 course, was a noncredited course of study, also labeled the school of hard knocks, which extended from 1929 to 1941. There was no college or university that listed this course in its curriculum posting. I wasn't the smartest kid in the world, but even at that early age I understood why it was necessary for my dad to work those long hours six days a week, why those hobos knocked on our front door, and why folks stood in that long line at the soup kitchen. My friends and I figured we had to follow our dads' leads and put "working" as number one on our life agenda, the rule of the day. It was clear to me that working meant money in the pocket keeping us far distant from that watered-down soup kitchen. In later life, I also came to the realization that an empty savings account would result in a financially lean retirement life. Simply stated, the Depression taught me that work wasn't a privilege; it was a necessity!

At fourteen years old, with that work ethic fresh in my mind, I bravely went looking for a job that summer. I applied for a job at the Lexington Baseball Park, home of the Saint Paul Saints AAA baseball team, just four blocks from my home. I was hired on the spot. It gave me a true feeling of importance when they issued me that white coverall uniform with the name "Saints" printed boldly on the back. This job offered an interesting work schedule. I began work at 8:00 a.m. cleaning the grandstand till 10:00 a.m.; from 10:00 a.m. till 3:00 p.m., we had free time. At three we prepared the playing field for the evening game. After dinner, I returned at 6:00 p.m. to retrieve foul balls during batting practice. During the game we were assigned to different stations in the ball park with responsibility for retrieving all baseballs that left the playing field. I was home by ten or at times eleven when games went into extra innings. Baseballs in those days were considered valuable ingredients that were to be returned to the field at all costs. In today's world, these balls apparently have little value and are given away freely. Maybe today, baseballs are cheaper than hiring groundskeepers! The initial lesson I learned at the Lexington Ball Park was that having money in your pocket could buy all those things I wanted without asking my dad for cash. With that $1.80 earned each day, I could buy all the White Castle hamburgers, Pepsi Cola, and ice cream I wanted, and I did. My dad could never figure out where all my money went. I was scared to tell him it was stashed away in my stomach. The exciting feature about working at the ball park was the opportunity to play ball on this professional baseball diamond during that 10:00 a.m. to 3:00 p.m. free time. There were times we actually worked out with the players. Wow, what a job! That was the very beginning of my work career. I realized that without cash in my pocket, I was "dead in the water." No way was I ever going to stand in that soup line.

The Depression had taught me the value and importance of working and the realization that the more I worked meant the more "things" I could purchase. Saving money apparently wasn't on my to-do list quite yet. I also learned in those early years that it's possible to have two jobs if they didn't conflict with each other. The second job I picked up at the ball park was shining the ball players' shoes for extra cash plus a bonus, a free baseball or two. Working at more than one job began early and was a work pattern I followed throughout my long work career. My dad's strong work ethic had apparently carried over to me. Anyway, these jobs were fun!

You can learn some very interesting things by working in a variety of different part-time jobs. For example, at the ballpark I learned a brand-new language from those ballplayers who joined the Saints team from all over the country. It was called swearing. I honestly believe my mother would never have allowed me to work at the ballpark if she knew the colorful, profane language used by those ballplayers. It didn't really change my language vocabulary because if I decided to adopt that language at home I would have been banned for life to the cellar with a bar of soap in my mouth. The winter job I later held with the city public works department was also educational. I was assigned to a dump truck loaded with sand to be spread on those icy streets after a snowstorm. I quickly learned that shoveling that sand made all those city workers on my truck thirsty and required regular stops at local beer joints to quench their thirst. It was interesting because I really was never that thirsty. The next summer I found a job with an asphalt company making alleys. They assigned me the job of "cook" but not in a restaurant. This job consisted of "cooking" up batches of tar to a boiling point. This tar was then used as the glue base for laying the asphalt. It was a hot, sweaty, miserable job that I discovered was always given to the new employee. I figured this was the job they used to test new employees to see who was worth keeping. I don't know if I passed the test or not because I had to return to school, thank God! It also was an interesting job because every time I looked up, the boss seemed to be watching me. I figured either I was doing a lousy job, or he was really impressed with my high-quality work performance. Then there was the job I secured in the summer of 1948 tearing out the floorboards of the bridge that towered high above the Mississippi River in Saint Paul. This bridge was high enough for planes to fly under, and with each board I tore out I feared for my life. I was absolutely frightened of heights, so it was either quit the job or have a nervous breakdown. To avoid the cost of those psychiatric sessions, I decided to quit. This taught me an important lesson: avoid all jobs ten feet above the ground. Another job I had during high school was working at the Gold Medal Beverage Company. I was assigned to the beverage assembly line with the task of removing six bottles at a time, giving them a big shake, then placing them in a carton for delivery to stores. We were given permission to drink all the pop we wanted. After two days of drinking more than my share of warm pop, I vowed to never drink another bottle of pop for the rest of my life. In my job at the South Saint Paul Grain Exchange I learned some workers can really be cruel. One of the workers had a stomach problem that was activated when something negative was mentioned about food. When the word got out to his coworkers, he was fair game and was forced to eat alone. The workers thought it was funny to talk about bugs in food and other negative food topics that forced this guy to dispose of his lunch. By the way, I didn't buy into their enjoyment. Working at this variety of jobs certainly was an educational experience. These laboring jobs, believe it or not, all contributed in some way to enhancing my work career. I learned something new at each job and wouldn't have missed any of these varied work opportunities for the world. I encourage everyone to experience a variety of jobs early in their work career, not only to increase your income but to enhance your education. You learn academics in college but you learn street smarts right in the trenches—the job. I honestly believe I learned more about working, and what it takes to be a successful employee in those "trenches" then at the university. Maybe the university should offer a course entitled Working!

I mention these early part-time job experiences because in addition to making extra cash, they helped open my eyes as to what work was all about, helped me learn some tricks in securing a job, taught me some hands-on work skills, helped improve my interactions with coworkers and management, and, most important of all, clued me in on those jobs to be avoided at all costs. I observed those employees who were the hard workers and wanted to advance on the job, those others satisfied to just hang with the status quo, and those who worked hardest to avoid work, and also those who were unhappy and dissatisfied with their job status and weren't bashful to share their feelings. These early jobs taught me quickly that a worker's attitude toward the job was the key factor in determining job satisfaction and advancement potential. The workers who appeared to enjoy their job, worked hard, and got along with coworkers and management were the ones who seemed always to get the better assignments, salary increases, and promotions. By the way, I absolutely loved my first job as a groundskeeper and might have stayed there permanently after leaving high school if the pay wasn't so low. Those two jobs of working for that asphalt company and on the high bridge were the pits. They were valuable, however, because they helped identify the work I should avoid at all costs. I learned that every job, including the lousy ones, teaches you something. My dad was instrumental in getting me these two lousy jobs. I wouldn't be surprised if this was his subtle way of letting me know some college or vocational training might be the best approach in planning my future. Well, his plan worked because I sure didn't like "cooking" or hanging by my fingertips from that high bridge. Thanks, Dad, for enhancing my education. I suggest that all young folks, early in their work career, follow the approach of getting as many job experiences as possible. What you learn in those early experiences will enhance your work career in the future, whether you have set your sights on a college education or not. Just avoid working on the high bridge!

Making a Decision
Develop a vocational plan of action.

Okay, so now I had at least a taste of what the world of work offered and, during the summer of 1948, after graduating from high school and working at these varied jobs, made the decision that getting some type of skill training was the direction I should take. I also understood that having a skill usually led to an increased income, which raised my interest level. I didn't want to be a machinist like my dad or pursue any of those summer job experiences ... except that ballpark job. I did enjoy my high school career, especially the music and sports activities, and the coach was my hero, so the possibility of becoming a teacher and coach did appeal to me. This occupation, however, would require attending college for the next four years, and none of my friends and no one in our family ever attended college. I figured college was only for those smart students, and I didn't consider myself in that category—hard worker, yes, but smart, no! I feared college might be beyond my ability level, and to participate and compete in that setting was a different story. In short, attending college scared me to death. The easy way out was to just go find a job, because my confidence level to attend college was at rock bottom, but I had to do something!

Hamline University was probably the easiest school for me to attend because I knew some friends already attending this school, and it was right in my neighborhood. On the other hand, I just loved baseball, and the university had an ex-major-league player as the coach, so attending the university was another possibility. The university, however, was so big, a long way from my home, and its national academic reputation scared me to death. A few days later, in a moment of weakness and in total fear, I made the fatal decision and registered at the university. Playing baseball for this Big Ten school was the clincher! I was very nervous and uptight as I followed what I considered to be a very complicated registration process that sent me from one building to another. I became so frustrated and discouraged with this complexity that I remember saying to myself, *If they send me to one more building, I'm going to head home and simply go out and find a job and take the easy way out.* I was seriously willing to hang it all up—to give up—and ready to walk away. Well, thank the Lord, they didn't send me to one more building, and that did it. I joined the big "M"!

I was walking into probably the biggest challenge of my life—a challenge never faced by any of my friends or members of my family. Now could I produce? As I picked up my books ready for that first day of class, I had little confidence that I could make it through the initial fall quarter. I figured if I couldn't hack the coursework, I would leave school, go find a job, and at least be able to tell friends and family that I attended the university. Well, to make a long story short, I made it through that first quarter, the second quarter, and all those remaining fourteen quarters. I graduated with good grades, got a wonderful education, and, yes, I did play on the baseball team, and to my surprise was named captain my senior year. Taking that chance, the gamble of my life, to get that college education had paid off. Apparently, I wasn't as dumb as I thought and remember telling my mother, "Maybe the university isn't just for those really smart kids after all!"

I mention my university experience only because the decision to attend was such a traumatic experience for me. This lack of confidence in myself, my fear of failure—that I'm simply not competent, capable, or possess the ability to handle the challenges of college—almost did me in. Accepting this challenge absolutely changed my life and future work career. I seriously question if I would be sitting comfortably in my retirement rocking chair today if I had taken the easy way out. It's so easy to not take the chance—to walk away! There are so many decisions, so many challenges in our lives that will affect our future. My advice to the reader is simple. Be willing to accept life's challenges head-on and not succumb to those fears of failure so many of us have. Don't be willing to accept a future of mediocrity. To maximum your income level and to live the good life leading to an enjoyable retirement will require you to gamble a bit, to "take a chance," along with a willingness to sacrifice. Remember, those folks who made it through that Great Depression did a lot of sacrificing to survive. It was their example that played a part in my decision to give the university a try. Maybe my decision to take a chance can be your incentive!

Beginning a Profession
Begin your career with enthusiasm and a willingness to multitask.

I walked out of the university a totally different person than when I entered. I transitioned from that shy, frightened person with little self-confidence to a person with goals, a new direction in life, and a readiness to take on whatever the world had to offer. Simply stated, I learned that winning the battle, achieving a goal I didn't think was possible, does wonders for your confidence level. That summer after graduation, I was offered a teaching job in one of Saint Paul's private high schools and the exciting opportunity to be the athletic director and coach. My career goal was to become a teacher/coach, and, by gosh, it was going to happen. As I look back, I often wonder what avenue, what direction in life, I would have taken if my decision had been to take the easy way out and never attend the university. How different my life might have been if, perish the thought, the university had sent me to just one more building to register. I would have given up and walked away from my dream job and, who knows, probably spread asphalt for the rest of my life. Take an old man's advice, and don't walk away from your dream, whatever it may be, no matter what roadblocks stand in your way! I can't stress that point enough.

I was twenty-three years old, fresh out of school, and reported to that teaching/coaching job at Saint Agnes High School a month before my official starting date and not yet on the payroll. I would be teaching five classes a day and was head coach in all three major sports: football, basketball, and baseball. Football practice began two weeks before school opened, so I had a lot to do before football practice ever began. My assistant coach was the shop teacher, the only other man on the faculty, who I soon learned never played football. I prepared the playbook, ordered some more uniforms, painted a white stripe down the top of each helmet to pep them up a bit, hired some officials, and was on my way. If the principal had asked me to wash the uniforms, I probably would have done that as well. You know, it's absolutely amazing what you do when you are the boss, there's no one telling you what to do, and apparently "common sense" is your guide. This is where those street smarts gained from my many work experiences really paid off. I must have done something right because in that first year as football coach, the Saint Agnes Aggies finished the season undefeated. Years later, this championship team was honored in the school's Hall of Fame. I remember the principal calling me in her office after this winning season and saying, "Mr. Schultz, it isn't always going to be this way." I found out quickly that she was absolutely right. I loved classroom teaching, and being head coach (really, the only coach) was beyond my fondest dreams.

When that first school year ended, I thought I had performed well and deserved a raise in salary. I met with the monsignor who was school superintendent and was told that money was tight, and a raise was impossible for next year and most likely for any future years. I was struggling financially on my $3,000 a year salary, and with a wife and child on the way my financial future looked bleak. I was earning less than a dollar an hour when I figured the many hours of coaching and extracurricular activities I was involved with. It was my dream job, but working almost free wasn't going to keep food on the table, and Spam wasn't my favorite meal. That unwritten teachers' rule book said you should always stay at least two years on the job, so I signed a contract for my second year. I knew teaching/coaching was my future, so after my second year, I planned to resign and locate a job in a suburban or rural community where the salary in public schools was much better. I suspect that my experience in entering the working world isn't a whole lot different than for many young people today. You locate your first job with limited pay that can easily lead you into a financial hole hard to climb out of. Believe me, I was there and know of what I speak. Fortunately, aided by a frugal wife, we survived, kept our head above water, and avoided drowning in debt. What I desperately needed was some additional income to supplement this meager teacher/coach salary. Wow, I was a winning coach and couldn't get a raise. That's another example that life isn't always fair!

Life's Unexpected Hiccup
Be prepared; sometimes the best-laid plans can go astray.

At completion of my second year of teaching I submitted my resignation, figuring my future looked bright, and I would have little trouble locating a new teaching position. That's exactly when the "hiccup" in my life occurred. My son became very ill and was diagnosed with an incurable genetic disability requiring extensive medical care and eventual hospitalization. Our doctors urged us to remain in the Saint Paul community so our son could receive the treatment he needed. We agreed to follow the doctor's advice, requiring me to put my teaching career on hold and seek other employment. Fortunately I had secured some part-time weekend work at the Saint Paul Police Department that provided a very minimal income. It looked like my problem was solved when I was offered a teaching position for the upcoming fall with the Saint Paul School System that should have solved my employment dilemma, but it didn't. I learned that the job was to teach science and mathematics, two subjects I was not qualified to teach, and, to be honest, my weakest subjects in school. To take that job would have been unfair to the students, so I said thanks and turned it down. How could I have accepted that job when I thought the dipper was something you used to scoop up water, and those fancy diagrams in geometry were part of a crossword puzzle!

My hiccup became more like "hiccups" when we learned our second son and later our third son also were diagnosed with this terrible debilitating disease. So, what do we do? We were surviving on a part-time job with no teaching job available, forced to remain living in Saint Paul, and, oh yes, my family was falling apart. My mother's advice to us was "move on with your life; God will take care of you." I remember asking her, "When exactly is that going to happen?" It was the most frightening and depressing time in our young lives. We had lost our life's direction with an unknown future ahead of us. We still had to survive and pay our bills, especially those ever-increasing medical bills, and deal with the everyday reality of life. Well, we didn't go on welfare, didn't get a divorce, didn't turn to alcohol or drugs to solve our problem, and didn't just give up. What we did was roll up our sleeves, dig our heels in, and follow my mother's advice to "move on with our life." This is not a religious book, but I also have to add that apparently God did take care of us. He's probably the reason we survived and didn't face bankruptcy. Someday, in the future, I plan to ask him. We began to "think out of the box" in ways to get our lives back on track. It's an interesting story how we survived during that trying time and discovered a totally new direction in our lives.

These hiccups occurred during the very beginning years of our marriage. I have come to the conclusion after these eighty-eight-plus years of life's experiences that no one gets away free, that everyone in his or her life will be faced with one or more hiccups, and, yes, that includes you! So don't freak out when your hiccup occurs. How you deal with that hiccup will without question affect your family life, your emotional health, and most likely your work career. As you will see, my wife and I survived our hiccup. After our three children passed away, we were blessed with three wonderful adopted children, and our life did go on in a totally new positive direction. We were the lucky ones. When that hiccup occurs in your life, and it will, we encourage you to deal with it positively as well. Make your problem, your hiccup, an opportunity to improve your life instead of destroying your life. Don't hesitate to "think out of the box," to try a new approach for a solution. Follow my mother's advice, "Get on with your life." It certainly worked for us! Actually our hiccups opened up an entirely new world for us. My mother knew what she was talking about!

Surviving Life's Hiccups: Dual Incomes
When surviving on one income isn't enough, go for two incomes.

My interest in sports began way back in grade school when my dad and I would play catch with the baseball in front of our home by the hour. When I entered sixth grade I joined our grade school baseball and basketball teams and continued playing baseball, basketball, plus football throughout my high school career and continued playing baseball at the university. I suspect my baseball skills were enhanced working at the Saint Paul Saints AAA Lexington baseball park where I worked as a groundskeeper. Actually, my big sports break came immediately after I graduated from high school. I was recruited right out of high school to be the paid pitcher for the New Prague town team in the Minnesota River League. Town baseball was big in the 1940s and '50s. Every town wanted to be a winner, so they began paying one or more out-of-town players to improve their record. I was paid eighty-five dollars each Sunday when I pitched and fifty dollars on Wednesday evening when I played first base or in the outfield. I played on that town team all four summers while attending the university. In 1952, after I graduated, most of the local businesses that were financing these paid ballplayers apparently decided this was a waste of money, and this trend ended. At that point, whether I liked it or not, playing baseball was going to be just for enjoyment with cold beer and brats. But, who knows, I did have a pretty good curve ball that some team just might be ... there's always hope, you know!

As luck had it, during the second year of my teaching/coaching job I ran into some good luck when my dad informed me that the Saint Paul Police Department had a baseball team that played two games a year against the Minneapolis Police team, with proceeds from these games used for charitable purposes. It was a competitive series because each team wanted to win. My dad said the Saint Paul Police team needed a pitcher. Having pitched at the university and in out state ball, I decided to offer my services. I called for an appointment with the chief of police, had an interview and was hired on the spot. The chief informed me there was one catch; I had to be an employee of the police department to be a team member. I desperately needed extra income so jumped at the opportunity to supplement my limited teaching/coaching salary. The chief assigned me to the department's Records Division to work weekends, selected evenings, and during my summer vacation. He asked if I had any typing training, and with tongue in cheek I told him I was a skilled typist. I got a C in my high school typing class taken five years previously, so I exaggerated a bit. I needed this job! Fortunately, my police work schedule didn't conflict with my teaching/coaching job, but it certainly played a part in making for a busy workweek. It was interesting to note that the hourly pay in this part-time police job was better than my hourly pay as a teacher/coach. By the way, these police baseball games were discontinued after two years.

With no job on the horizon after resigning from Saint Agnes, and my teaching/coaching career put on hold because of the medical needs of my sick children, I asked the chief if I could become a full-time employee, and he agreed. Wow, I wasn't going on welfare after all! If you are curious how my pitching career turned out with the Saint Paul Police team, I am happy to report that I was the winning pitcher in all four games. I think this winning record played an important part in their decision to make me a full-time employee. When I went on this full-time schedule at the police department, I was given permission to work whenever I was available and pretty much whenever I wanted. They were short of help and falling behind in the Records Division's ever-increasing workload. In 1955, while employed full time, I worked all 365 days, and some of these were ten-hour days. During the summer, when the baseball games were played, they paid extra for our practice time and for each game, plus gave us two days of extra bonus pay. Believe it or not, that summer I was the highest-paid worker on the police force, making more than the chief of police. When this was discovered, I was asked to reduce my time a bit but was told, "Keep on working; we need you!" It was interesting that this entry-level typing job in the police Records Division paid a better hourly wage than my teaching/coaching job. Just think, four years at the university to become a glorified typist. Wow, life really isn't fair!

I saved hardly a nickel of this police income. We were keeping up with the payments on those ever-increasing medical bills and during this time purchased our first home, paid our mortgage payment right on schedule, and fortunately didn't go hungry. Thankfully, we somehow were able to remain out of debt. This police job was an absolute lifesaver and kept us in a survival mode. Without that police department job, I suspect we might still be floundering in debt, most likely living a very frugal life. It turns out I was sort of the relief pitcher for the police Records Division. I want to thank my dad for playing catch with me all those years because playing baseball really paid off for me. But who ever thought it would lead to police work?

Officiating: Another Income Source
If one income isn't enough, add a second income source.

While in high school I took part in both our high school's music and athletic programs and was active in other school activities as well. This participation made my high school years fun and exciting and led to my continued involvement in sports activities at the university as well. Let's face it, my participation on the university baseball team certainly paid an important part in helping to secure that key police department job. In my fondest dreams, to be employed by the police department, and be the pitcher on their baseball team, was never on my life's agenda. I figured if the New York Yankees or the Minnesota Twins didn't want to sign me for a big bonus, the police department would just have to do.

I absolutely loved my two years of teaching and coaching, but if my coaching career was finished, then I decided to give officiating basketball and football a try. I figured this was the best way to continue smelling those sweaty locker rooms without spending time hollering at my players. This officiating occupation worked out well, and for the next thirty-seven years kept me on the athletic field plus earning an additional income. The money earned from officiating was minimal but a welcome supplement to my police department salary, particularly during the early 1950s when the police department was my primary source of income, and my medical expenses were excessive. It offered an important second income source.

It's interesting how my officiating career began. In my junior year at the university, being a physical education major, I was asked by the intramural director if I would be interested in officiating intramural basketball games. I accepted his request and discovered it was an activity I really enjoyed and gave me the satisfaction of being part of the basketball scene. As luck had it in my senior year, and even after graduation, I was offered the opportunity to officiate all the Minneapolis Lakers preliminary basketball games at the Minneapolis Auditorium. To watch the world champion Minneapolis Lakers led by the great George Miken was the thrill of a lifetime, and that two-dollar paycheck was a true bonus. Late in my senior year at the university, I was also hired to officiate Catholic Athletic Association (CAA) senior basketball games played in Saint Paul on Sunday afternoons. My partner and I officiated three games every Sunday afternoon, also for the grand total of two dollars a game. It was fun and was a great experience. Remember, two dollars went a lot further in those early 1950s. If you could handle the pressure of these games, you then were given the opportunity to officiate in the Saint Paul City Senior Basketball League. This was big money—three dollars a game. But you earned every nickel of it. Those city league games were rough and tumble, and to be threatened with your life was often a common occurrence. If you could handle these games and make it out unscathed, you "passed the test" and were eligible to join the Saint Paul Officials Association, ready for assignment to state high school games and hopefully to the big league—those Minnesota State College games!

This stepping-stone process in the officiating world sounds easy, but believe me there were many challenges along the way; however, it was exciting and a way of making some much-needed extra money. I recall working one Saint Paul Senior League basketball game when by the third quarter we had fouled out three members of the Jackson's Bar team, and the game had to be called for lack of players. When this game abruptly ended, I felt eminent danger to my life and made the wise decision to avoid showering and headed immediately to my car in record speed. I can still hear the footsteps following me from many irate fans and players. Interestingly enough, the next evening this same Jackson's Bar team was scheduled to play the preliminary game to the Minneapolis Lakers before a crowd of thousands at the huge Minneapolis Auditorium. Playing before this large crowd must have had some leveling effect on improving both the Jackson's team skill and emotional level, because they played basketball instead of gym football. The night before we were the enemy, ready to be tarred and feathered, barely escaping from the gym with our lives, but on this night we all were good friends as we shook hands and heard the term "nice game." As the enemy, I made three dollars and as "good friends" I made two dollars. Again, life just isn't fair! The pay wasn't much, but the excitement of the game was worth it!

After graduation from the university and while still involved in my high school coaching career, I joined the Saint Paul Officials Association and was assigned to officiate both high school football and basketball games throughout Wisconsin and Minnesota and in later years joined the college ranks. In those early years, officials were paid five dollars to work high school B basketball game and ten dollars for the A game. If I remember correctly, in 1987 when I retired my officiating jersey we were paid ten dollars for the B game and twenty-five dollars for the A high school game and between fifty and seventy-five dollars for a college game. Today high school officials earn close to one hundred dollars or more a game, with college officials earning well over that figure. Obviously I was born too soon!

During my two-year stint of coaching at Saint Agnes, I had to fit in an officiating schedule that didn't conflict with my coaching schedule. By careful scheduling I still managed to work a decent number of games. After leaving Saint Agnes and joining the police department, I was able to officiate a full football and basketball schedule. Believe me, that supplemental income source came in handy. In my heyday of officiating, I would generally work three basketball games a week, with my pay each week totaling about one hundred dollars. In football, I worked on an average of two games a week, earning about the same amount. As mentioned, with my high school coaching career behind me, this money was a valuable supplement to my police department income to help cover those increasing medical expenses. Although this second income was a plus, it was something I thoroughly enjoyed. I looked forward to the excitement and challenge of each game. There also was a negative side effect. In the 1960s and '70s, my heyday of officiating, I was away from home and the family a considerable amount of time and missed many family events and my children's sporting activities that were taking place in our home community. Later in my career I did take my boys to a few games that I officiated, but with their school and sports schedule that wasn't always possible. I regret the fact that I did miss many of their football and baseball games and my daughters' diving meets. My wife was very supportive to my officiating activities and never objected to my being away from home because this extra money was a real bonus. She recognized our family's need for this added income to keep us debt free, enhance our future, and improve our lifestyle. Fortunately we both were singing off the same song sheet. We may not have been an officiating team, but we certainly were a "family team."

Years later, after retiring from officiating, I asked my children if my extended time away from home was a problem for them. They all said absolutely not. I had followed the practice of bringing home Bridgeman's ice cream malts after each game I officiated and placed these malts in the freezer when I arrived home. By morning when they woke up, these frozen malts would be waiting for them to be enjoyed as they watched their morning TV shows. My daughter said, "Dad, we loved it when you were gone, so we could have those delicious frozen malts." Who knows, maybe they would have liked me to officiate four or even five games a week. Ah, the benefits of bribery. For my wife and me it meant no debts and a better living style!

Music: An Income Source
If two income sources aren't enough, add a third.

In many Minnesota high schools, students are faced with the decision to either participate in sports or to play in the band. Many school administrators and coaches decided that you simply can't do both. In my high school era, I somehow became the rare exception. It just happened that I became active in both extracurricular activities without the knowledge of the coach or music director, and when they discovered my dual involvement it was too late to do anything about it. I ended up playing football, basketball, and baseball and at the same time played in nearly all band activities including concerts, parades, and assemblies, and in my senior year was elected president of the band. Yes, you guessed it, I didn't play in the band at football games. I could have played during halftime, but then I would have missed our football coaches' stimulating halftime pep talks! The only time I ran into trouble with this dual schedule was one Friday evening when our German band (Sauerkrauts) played at halftime for a 6:30 p.m. high school basketball game at the Hamline University arena. I was the starting guard for our high school basketball team that was scheduled to play the third game that evening. The basketball coach saw me playing the tuba prior to our game, and he was livid. He figured playing the tuba would tire me out for our 9:00 p.m. game. He said some nasty things to me. Actually, I didn't play bad that evening and was high scorer, but we still lost by twenty points. That sort of took the pressure off. To be perfectly honest, I think playing the tuba increased my wind capacity and improved my playing skills. Unfortunately, the basketball coach had tunnel vision and little interest in music. He failed to see the full picture!

I'm not sure Doc Raymond, our band instructor, or Bill Fitzharris, our football and baseball coach, liked my dual interests, but they were friends and apparently "peace" did prevail between them. This certainly worked to my personal benefit because this dual sports/music participation in high school offered the early incentive to eventually become a high school coach, to officiate in the Minnesota sports arena, and to also participate in the local music scene ... all extra moneymakers. If the high school administration had limited my opportunity to only playing sports, or to only be in the band, they may well have curtailed my future part-time income opportunities. These earnings didn't make me a millionaire, but they offered a steady side income that helped pay off those initial medical bills, purchase the extras in life, and eventually add to our retirement savings account. Who said high school isn't important in preparing for a career?

In addition to playing in our high school band, we also formed a German polka band called the Sauerkrauts made up of several band members. This was purely a band for fun and enjoyment although we did win a couple of music contests. All this led up to my joining a seventeen-piece dance band in my senior year. I made my first two dollars in the John Baskerville and Hounds band playing for a high school gig in 1948. This was the beginning of a music career that has spanned some seventy years and allowed me to participate in approximately ten different music groups of all types—1940s big dance bands, small combos, polka old-time bands, jazz bands, and music variety bands. I currently am leader of the Hi Hat band that plays for senior dances and entertains at nursing homes and retirement centers and other local events. Music has proven to be an enjoyable hobby and another wonderful supplement to our family income. Musicians are not paid particularly well, but fifty dollars here and one hundred dollars there tends to add up. In those challenging 1950s, money from band gigs and officiating helped keep us out of debt. In the 1960s through the 1990s these supplemental income sources bought me things I couldn't normally afford and beefed up our savings account. During my retirement years this music income has been used for fun vacations and regular dinner dates with the wife. It's fun in these latter years to act like a big spender!

When I left that teaching/coaching job in 1954, I hit rock bottom. My coaching career had abruptly ended, my three children were critically ill and eventually passed away, the hospital bills were immense, and for a time we were surviving on my part-time job. We were facing deep financial troubles. In a way, we were facing the same uphill financial struggle that many young folks are facing today when they enter the working world in heavy debt and facing those high cost of living expenses. I was forced to "think out of the box" to locate other income sources. My baseball background allowed my part-time job to go full time at the police department, my basketball and football experiences brought additional income by expanding my officiating schedule, and my music gigs offered another income supplement when I needed it the most. These multiple income sources kept us out of debt and able to live a normal life under some pretty dire circumstances, particularly in those challenging 1950s. I suggest you take a moment and review your own life experiences and see what supplemental income possibilities you may have. Your regular income will most likely allow for your survival needs, but it's identifying another supplemental income source (or sources) that will speed up reducing your debts and hasten the time leading to financial independence. So sit back and try to figure out what supplemental source (or sources) of income might be available to you, particularly in your interest areas. I'm convinced using supplemental income is one of the best ways to move ahead financially. If this income source (or sources) is in your interest area, then it isn't just work; it can be fun! I happened to just luck out and came up with two supplemental income sources that both were in my interest areas. With these added income sources, we stayed financially above water, and when our personal life straightened out, we were on our way!

Supplemental Income Sources
Identify your potential supplemental income sources.

Keep in mind the premise that developing a positive financial plan early in your work career is your goal, and the earlier the better. A supplemental job is an excellent way for you to accumulate extra income; it certainly was beneficial for me. The timing and frequency of this part-time job, of course, can't conflict with your regular job, and the spouse or partner better agree with this added time away from home, or there may be trouble brewing. There are many part-time jobs available in the community, but to find one that fits a person's interest area should be top priority. I was fortunate in using my sports and music background as additional income sources. Another example would be a policeman handling traffic control in funeral processions, a teacher providing tutorial reading, or an accountant handling the books for a small business, and the list goes on and on. It's up to you to identify what part-time venture within your interest areas might be available.

In the late 1980s I designed my family home but used a local draftsman who did private work on the side to actually draw the plan to scale. A local cement worker who took side jobs on weekends constructed all my sidewalks and two patios. A carpenter friend used his days off and weekends away from his regular job to help construct my sun room. My office cabinets and desk were built and installed by a retired cabinet worker who took side jobs as a supplement to his Social Security income. My outdoor yard lighting was designed and done by a fellow who worked for a lighting company and wanted work on the side to secure enough cash to start his own company. These were all fully capable and trained workers, but they wanted to supplement their income just like me. I quickly learned that their bids were always far lower than those of company bids, so as a result I saved a considerable amount of money on these building projects as well. Each of these tradesmen benefited financially by this side income that didn't have to be shared with others. I'm sure this side money was put to good use by each of these tradesmen. Maybe at this point you are saying, "But won't having a second job cut into my social or golf time?" The answer to this question is very simple. "Yes, it probably will, but if you begin making this extra income early in your career, you just may be able to pay off your debts and get on solid financial ground so in future years you can golf, party, or fish to your heart's content. Plan early; play later! The next step is up to you!

Changing Occupations in Midstream
Turn a problem into an opportunity.

After Michael, my first son, became ill, and during the time I was employed at the police department, our family physician suggested we join a newly formed cerebral palsy organization in Saint Paul. He felt it would serve as sort of a support group because it was apparent Michael would need long-term care. It was helpful to meet with other parents that also had children with serious disabilities. With the increased knowledge gained from this organization I soon became acquainted with the many helping and support services available to individuals and families with disabilities in the community. It was from my involvement with this organization that I learned of a brand new federal program, titled Vocational Rehabilitation, that was formed to assist folks with disabilities secure vocational training and find employment. I discovered that this new program was structured as a new division within the State Department of Education and was advertising for counselor positions. With no teaching or coaching job in sight, and because this program operated as part of the Department of Education, and me being an educator, I decided to throw my hat in the ring. I picked up a brochure that described this position and some of the job duties and responsibilities but didn't bother to do any further investigation before taking the required test for this position. This was a huge mistake because the test was focused almost entirely on psychological theory and counseling techniques that were totally out of my realm of knowledge, with not one question on the theory of sports. It was truly disappointing when I learned I had failed the test. A few days later, however, I did receive a call from the program's assistant director to come in for a second interview. The assistant director had previously been a football coach, and we hit it off very well in our initial interview. He said he liked my background and offered me the rehabilitation counselor job if I would agree to return to the university to take some additional psychology courses and be willing to begin work as a trainee at a reduced rate of pay. I needed a permanent job so enthusiastically agreed with these terms and walked into a brand-new career. To be perfectly honest, I believe it was my coaching experience that got me that job. Thank God again for my sports background.

Wow, good-bye teaching and coaching! I just walked into a brand spanking new career. I was to receive this trainee wage so decided to keep working at the police department on weekends and continued blowing my referee whistle and taking on music gigs. I still needed these three supplemental jobs to keep my financial head above water. By the way, I recently read in the business section of the Minneapolis paper that in today's world it's not unusual for a worker to be employed in as many as four different occupations before retirement. It appears I was on my way to make this prediction come true. If any reader needs a used football playbook, let me know!

Starting from Scratch
Past work experiences are beneficial in most future jobs.

This Vocational Rehabilitation position was an entirely new career for me. I discovered it was also a new experience for the other employees as well because federal legislation for this program had been passed just the previous year. These other newly employed counselors all had the psychology and counseling training that the job description required. My coaching background made me sort of a misfit in this profession, but I planned to get up to speed as quickly as possible by taking those required psychology courses at the university. On the other hand, I felt my diversified working background, which most of these counselors didn't have, was in my favor. My experience at the police department taught me the full range of clerical tasks that were required for this job along with skills in dictating and note taking. I also felt my police department experience in gaining information from the public would be an asset. My many past job experiences taught me to deal comfortably with a wide variety of individuals from all walks of life. Officiating taught me to work under pressure and to handle conflict with a cool head. As a coach, I learned to be a leader, make decisions, and motivate individuals, plus a willingness to take direct action. Being a parent of disabled children, I learned patience and a better understanding of disability, plus a commitment to improve conditions for individuals with disabilities. So it's true, I walked into this new position lacking some of the required counseling skills but, on the other hand, I had acquired what I call street smarts, something that really was an asset in this new job. This is an argument in favor of your getting as many work experiences in your employment background as possible.

Looking back on this career change, I understood that vocational counseling was the hallmark of this job in helping individuals prepare for work. Where I differed from certain of my fellow counselors was in the action needed in the follow-up after job decisions were reached. If finding a certain job was the objective reached through counseling, I felt a personal responsibility to aggressively leave my office, hit the streets, and help find that job if the more traditional approaches to seeking work weren't successful. In contrast, most counselors relied solely on other agencies for job placement responsibilities. I believe my more aggressive job-seeking approach led to more successful placements, particularly with severely disabled clients, rather than handing off that responsibility to others. This job proved to be challenging, exciting, and very rewarding, but my counseling office did lack that sweaty locker room smell that coaching offered.

Qualities Needed for Advancement
A willingness to take a chance leads to promotions and increased income.

Up to this point I've emphasized the importance of using supplemental work as a valuable means of increasing your income to help eliminate those nonproductive debts, to enhance future life and career planning, and to begin building a savings program. There is an additional approach to increasing your income level as well called "advancement," by taking advantage of promotion opportunities within your current company or promotional vacancies with other companies. Remember, promotions always mean more money in your pocket, and that's your goal. In addition to the technical skills required for a leadership position, there are certain personal skills that employers look for as well. Let's review a few of these personal skills.

I was employed as a rehabilitation counselor for a little over a year when, to my surprise, I was offered the position of director of vocational services at the Sister Kenny Institute in Minneapolis. This was a high-level management position with considerable responsibility in one of America's leading polio centers. Apparently, I must have done something right in my short duration as a rehabilitation counselor.

I think my counseling style and more aggressive approach to job placement had caught the attention of certain folks in this field. My initial reaction was to turn this job down because of my lack of experience and training. I jokingly told the Kenny Institute director who interviewed me that I was so new in this field I still hadn't learned to spell *rehabilitation*. My position with the state was very secure with fringe benefits and a decent but not great salary, so why leave for a job in the private sector offering a far more insecure future? My conservative father would have felt the same way—like father like son. The pay would be much better, which interested me, but I questioned my ability to handle this position, and this lack of security worried me. My damn conservative attitude and lack of confidence still was rearing its ugly head. I was facing a real dilemma. Should I take on this new unknown challenge or remain with the comfortable and secure position the state job offered? I was so distraught and frightened about facing this challenging decision that I couldn't sleep at night and was an absolute nervous wreck. I honestly wondered if this job was simply beyond my skill level. Remember the anxieties and fears of failure I expressed before I registered at the university? Well, they returned only a bit more intense. It would have been so easy to not take the chance, turn down this offer, and remain in my comfortable and secure position with the state. I thought back to those earlier Depression days wondering if I was working on one of those secure government WPA jobs, would I be willing to leave for a better but far less secure job in industry? Well, in a moment of weakness, I decided to take the Kenny Institute job, feeling I was probably gambling my life away.

All that worrying was for nothing because the Kenny Vocational Program helping folks with disabilities prepare for work took off like gangbusters, and in just a two-year period the program had outgrown our work area with a client waiting list. This program was expanded into a building next door to the institute, allowing us to service both Kenny polio and stroke inpatients plus individuals with a wide array of disabilities being referred on a statewide basis. After experiencing this success, I began to define myself as a gambler on a hot winning streak! Wow, Dad, what's happening to my conservative upbringing? The moral is simple; I'll say it again, "Be willing to take a chance!" Don't let yourself hide in the weeds. Get out and chase your dream.

That job change, or the new promotion that is frightening you to death, may just be the opportunity offering new exciting challenges and, in addition, fatten your savings account, and that's your goal! Remember the story of the train fighting its way up the hill saying, "I think I can; I think I can." Well, so can you if you are willing to take the chance!

I remember asking my mother in her later years if there was anything she regretted doing in her life that she wished could be changed. She said, "Yes, there was one thing I would have done differently, and it has bothered me all these years." She went on to explain the incident, and I remember it well. I was a senior in high school and on Friday asked to use the family car for a Saturday night date, and my mother gave approval. My older brother, who was in the navy, surprised us with an unscheduled visit home on that very Friday evening. She recalled how he had walked close to a mile from the streetcar to our home in subzero weather wearing only his light navy coat. Saturday morning he asked to use the family car that evening for a date, because he had to return the next morning to his base. She said, "I turned him down because I promised you the car. He had come all that way to visit us from Illinois, and I wouldn't let him even use the car. It was the mistake of my life." I told her she was all wrong, and that I was the guilty party. I should have offered him the car, what any good brother would have done. Just think, that event had bothered my mother for over seventy-five years. Don't let this happen to you. In future years don't find yourself looking back saying, "I should have taken that job or have applied for that promotion. Why was I so scared to take the chance? It was the mistake of my lifetime!" Someone once said that fear of failure is the anxiety that holds many of us back from creative ventures. Don't let that fear of failure cripple your life; be willing to take a chance. I often think back to how close I came to crippling my life!

With the confidence gained from my positive experience at the Elizabeth Kenny Institute, I decided to leave that position and accept an offer from the State Vocational Rehabilitation Agency to become supervisor of its Saint Paul Regional Office. After two years on this job, I was promoted to a state office consultant position and later became assistant to the director. Needless to say, with this rapid advancement under my belt, my confidence level was at its peak and, being in my midthirties, was ready for any new challenge. That challenge came in 1964 when the director of special education in the Saint Paul Public Schools asked me to join their staff as special education supervisor to develop a new service program that would better prepare students with disabilities for the world of work. I accepted this promotion and remained with the Saint Paul Schools till my retirement in 1993. Here's the point I'm trying to make. Leaving the security of a state position for the uncertainty of the Kenny Institute position opened the door to numerous job advancements, each offering salary increases. Keep in mind that I also was making a few bucks officiating football and basketball and continued to play in local bands all during my working career as well. The salary increases from these promotions plus these two sources of extra income meant money in the bank. At this point in my life, I was fully aware that retirement was creeping closer, and money in the bank was a necessity. I knew purchasing that retirement rocking chair wasn't going to be cheap!

Have you noticed how many professional football coaches began their initial coaching career at the high school level? A few with exceptional winning records find themselves hired for college or university football coaching positions. From the college and university ranks, a select few coaches with outstanding records are hired to join the professional coaching ranks. The interesting fact is that once coaches enter this elite professional coaching fraternity they nearly always remain in this high-level status whether they have a winning or a losing record. Some may become TV analysts, but most move from team to team in various coaching positions. They sort of become members of "the club." This trend is true not only in professional sports but in business and industry as well. It is not unusual to see CEOs regularly move from company to company even when they end up being fired. It appears that once you're in these elite positions, you apparently become a permanent member of this "club." The real challenge, of course, is to make it into that "club." This, in a way, is also true at the entry working level. What does it take to move from that beginning entry job to that team leader or supervisory position, where an increased salary enters the picture? In my case I moved into "the club" the day I took a chance and reported to work at the Kenny Institute. With that move I entered the management scene, opening the door for other management positions "the club" offered ... and more money. Some say advancing into "the club" is just luck, being at the right place at the right time, or knowing the right people, like when your dad is CEO of the company. They may have a point, but I'm convinced it's much more than that. Let me share an old man's feelings on this issue.

A Positive Attitude
A willingness to "go the extra mile" leads to promotions and extra income.

As a school administrator, there was an interesting saying when it came to hiring teachers: "If applicants came from a farm background, hire them; they have the best work ethic." I don't know if this motto holds true anymore because hardly anyone comes from a farm background today. Having a good work ethic, however, will always be one of the key factors in employing workers. You see, a good work ethic includes being a hard worker, being willing to take on needed tasks to enhance the company's performance, and contributing ideas to increase the company's productivity, plus being a loyal company employee. These are the qualities that employers look for when the time comes to select staff for promotional positions. In looking back, I believe there are two prominent reasons why certain workers are passed over for promotions. One reason is that the worker fails to apply for the promotion. He or she may have all the necessary qualifications but lack the confidence or feel he or she is not capable of performing the duties and responsibilities of the promotion. A worker may offer a dozen different excuses for not throwing his or her hat in the ring, but fear of the unknown is holding the person back. He or she is unwilling to take a chance. The salary increase is appealing, but the challenge is too great! The often-used excuse that the new job will take more time away from the family is simply a cover-up for fear. The second most common reason for rejection is that the worker's past performance record doesn't warrant the promotion. The salary increase is appealing, but for one reason or another the worker has not exhibited leadership potential. Don't allow yourself to fall into either of these negative categories if an increased salary is your goal. Let me share a few examples of these two points.

A good friend of mine was working in a social work position for a community agency. He was considered one of its top performers, and when the executive director left for another position, my friend was in line for this promotion. He appeared to have the necessary experience and qualifications for the job but turned down the promotion saying it would take too much of his personal time. If the truth be known, he really was scared off by the responsibilities of this job and decided he was not up for the challenge. He walked away from this wonderful opportunity because he was unwilling to take a chance! Today he is still employed as a case worker with little opportunity for any further advancement in that agency. He had all the necessary skills for this position but lacked the self-confidence and courage to make the move. Now, years later, he's forced to live with his decision, realizing he was probably the right person for that job. So, no confidence … no promotion … no salary increase!

In my working career, I've seen talented folks who expressed an interest to advance in their field but lacked the vitality or commitment to their current job and, as a result, were overlooked when promotion time came around. These individuals were comfortable with the status quo and were often critical of the company that employed them—their job duties, salary, etc. They hung in the weeds and were nowhere around when opportunities for improving job conditions or performance occurred. Frankly their interest in leadership positions was primarily for the salary increase. These folks were bypassed by management who instead were in search of leaders, motivators, and positive thinkers. Let me offer an example. Our school district was seeking to develop some new approaches in the development of job skills for youth with behavior problems. We were asking for volunteers to implement a newly developed pilot program to focus on this need. A few selected staff that had been with the district for many years sat on their hands when volunteers were requested. A couple of more energetic staff members, on the other hand, quickly raised their hands and enthusiastically offered to be involved in this pilot program, which involved additional work time. They were willing to explore a new approach, to take a chance, and see if this new pilot approach would benefit these students. These are the individuals employers seek out for leadership positions.

One of my former school administrators described the three levels of teachers she had worked with over the years. Group one, those teachers who were just willing to get by in their teaching assignments, who were unwilling to do anything extra, or take on any new assignments. Group two, those teachers who work hard to be good teachers, fully carry out their assignments, but were satisfied with their current status. Group three, those special teachers who were always trying to improve their teaching skills, willing to try new approaches and techniques in their classrooms, and possessed leadership ability in promoting educational growth. The teachers I described above, those willing to try something new, fit into the group three category. They were willing to take a chance and try some new approaches in improving services for this important student population. It doesn't take a Philadelphia lawyer to determine who the best promotional prospects are. School administrators seek out those group three teachers who exhibit school leadership potential and enthusiasm to lead. This same philosophy occurs in business and industry. Management wants leaders not complainers. Make sure you fit in that group three category if your objective is to climb the company ladder ... and an increased salary is your goal!

Being Persistent
Winners don't give up; losers do.

You work for this company and come up with what you feel is a great idea for improving production and saving the company money. You decide to share this idea with your boss. Halfway through your presentation he interrupts and says, "Thank you for your idea, but it will never work." What a letdown! Maybe your presentation was flawed, or you approached your boss on a bad day, or other more important issues were on his mind. You have two choices: dump your idea in the wastebasket or figure out a different approach to sell your plan. Maybe gaining the support of others will help, or writing the plan in detailed form for the boss's review when he has more time. It's up to you, and nobody else, to figure out a way to get his attention and hopefully change his mind. I remember my boss telling me, "Don't come to my office with three different ideas. It's too much. Come in with one idea that's well thought out, and then let's talk." It was good advice that made sense, and believe me I stored this advice away for future reference. It's so easy to accept rejection as gospel and toss your idea in the wastebasket. Too many people are willing to accept rejection, give up, and simply walk away. Don't fall into this "give up" category. Be persistent; don't be so willing to accept rejection; accept the challenge of winning the battle. The New England football team accepted that challenge. They were unwilling to give up when trailing by twenty points in the 2016 Super Bowl but fought back to win an overtime victory, and as a result walked away with the Super Bowl trophy, a fancy ring, and a truckload of cash! Being persistent, and using a different approach to get the boss's attention, may well benefit the company and very possibly mean a promotion for you. Yes, more money!

In the early 1960s, the State Vocational Rehabilitation Agency noted an increase of referrals from school districts of young adults with special needs who were ill prepared for entry into the world of work and many who were listed as school dropouts. The school curriculum was obviously not meeting the needs of these students. A number of us suggested a totally new approach to better prepare these students for the world of work. It was recommended that we assign selected vocational-rehabilitation-trained staff to work in partnership with special education teachers to enhance the school curriculum by placing more emphasis on job preparation and personal living skills. The director supported this idea, but no follow-up action occurred. One afternoon, the director asked if I would like to go with him to attend his son's football game. This gave me plenty of time, while driving to and from the game, to discuss this issue with no distractions. He liked the idea and asked me to write up a grant proposal to seek federal dollars to help implement this idea. I followed up on his suggestion, and, to our delight, this grant was approved along with federal funding for the project. These monies allowed us to hire vocation adjustment coordinators (VACs) to work in partnership with special education teachers right within the school setting. The project was to be piloted in the Saint Paul School District, and I was asked to leave my state position to implement and manage this project. The project proved to be very successful, resulting in a major reduction in the school dropout rate. As a result of this success, many Minnesota school districts followed suit and adopted this VAC program. By being persistent and not letting this idea die on the vine, a major educational change occurred. I'll say it again; don't give up on a good idea that you are convinced will benefit your work. The challenge you face is figuring out how to sell your idea to management. Maybe your boss won't ask you to attend a football game, but taking him to lunch might work. By the way, by being persistent, this idea resulted in my promotion and another salary increase.

Being Responsible
Follow through on your commitments.

Our High-Hat band was booked for an important dancing engagement. The very night before we were to perform, our keyboard player was hospitalized. Without a keyboard player, we would have to cancel this engagement. My immediate solution was to contact another musician who had played the keyboard with us and would be a competent replacement. I got panicky when he informed me that he had purchased expensive tickets to a musical performance that evening and would be unable to play. Now what to do? No other keyboard player had ever played with us. My first thought was to immediately cancel the job; that would be the easiest solution. I also was painfully aware that you couldn't have a dance without a band, and I didn't want to let the folks down that hired us. I thought for a moment trying to figure out an alternative solution. I remembered that a drummer we used on occasion also played the concertina, not a keyboard, but who knows, it might work out. I held my breath and called this fellow the evening before we were to play and learned he was available. I asked him to immediately email me a list of all the songs he knew. The next morning, I compared his song list with ours and made a new list of songs we mutually knew; however, we had never played these songs together. I emailed this new song list to him later that morning, and we agreed to meet at his home and run through each of these songs together. We met at one, and by four thirty had gone through each song. We packed up our instruments, fronts, and sound equipment, drove to the job, and were playing away at six thirty that evening. Everyone had a great time, and they seemed to love our music. The folks who hired us had no idea what trauma we went through to guarantee them music that evening. We didn't give up and walk away from our responsibility. We figured that the total time spent in preparing and playing for this gig earned us about $1.50 an hour, but we did it! We accomplished our goal and walked away with a well-deserved paycheck. We didn't give up and take the easy way out and as a result are still playing for this dance gig each month. We would have had some unhappy folks if we had backed out and, who knows, might well have ended our playing opportunity for their future dances. By being responsible, we are still on their monthly dance schedule making that one hundred dollars each gig. My message is simple; when you agree to a task, do it, no matter what obstacles you face. Don't settle for being a good loser; it's more gratifying to be a winner!

Join the Movement
Get involved in "community action" organizations; be a change agent.

When I began employment in 1956 as a rookie vocational rehabilitation counselor, Mary Sweeney, an older, experienced counselor, served as my job trainer and was most helpful teaching me the ropes of this new position. After a few months on the job she urged me to attend an evening dinner meeting for an organization called the Minnesota Rehabilitation Association (MRA). I was not very enthused to attend and pay the eight-dollar cost of this dinner, but to keep a good relationship with Miss Sweeney, I decided to attend. I met a number of people at this meeting employed in the many related fields of rehabilitation and picked up quite a bit of information plus made some new friends, and the food wasn't bad! I concluded that attending this meeting was beneficial in learning more about my work, was worth the eight dollars, and decided to keep attending each month. When the annual National Rehabilitation Association meeting was scheduled in Washington, DC, that upcoming summer, I also opted to attend along with other MRA members. This meeting helped provide the inside national picture of what rehabilitation was all about. I was meeting new folks in related fields; my learning curve was up, and my own reputation in the field was increasing. Mary Sweeney was right on target when she told me to get involved beyond the eight to four thirty workday. She said, "Don't just do your day job but participate and get active in those organizations and committees that can play a part in improving services to the disabled."

Mary Sweeney was a wonderful role model and excellent teacher. She not only put in a full day at the office but in evenings and on weekends would work from her dining room table at home. I bought into her "community action" philosophy completely and in time became president of the Minnesota Rehabilitation Association, president of the Midwest Regional Rehabilitation Association, chairman of the Saint Paul Mayors Committee on Employment of the Handicapped, and was active in numerous local and state committees that focused on developing equal opportunities for the disabled. This put me on the ground floor in working with others to help develop legislation to eliminate the many social, employment, and architectural barriers that folks with disabilities had to face. This related involvement in the rehabilitation field certainly helped to improve my status and credibility on the job. My community involvement, without question, was a major factor in being selected for that job at Kenny Institute over many more qualified counselors. This involvement also was an important factor in my later promotions within the State Vocational Rehabilitation Department. It wasn't a job anymore, it became a commitment! If the message hasn't sunk in yet, I'm telling you very clearly that those who do more, go beyond their job duties, and show an above-board commitment to their company or agency, are first in line for promotions. Bosses just love these kinds of workers! By the way, if you attended the Minnesota State Fair, did you observe the many folks in wheelchairs and walkers maneuvering with ease from building to building, the accessible bathrooms, special handicapped parking slots, plus other adaptations to make this event accessible for all? It was our Saint Paul Mayor's Advisory Committee, along with other organizations, that played a key role in making this state fair accessible to everyone. So roll up your sleeves and get involved; it'll pay off for you!

An interesting opportunity opened up for me in the early 1960s, again because of my community involvement. I was asked to join the board of directors of the Nevin Huested Foundation for Handicapped Children. This foundation provided financial grants to teachers, agencies, and organizations that served handicapped youth. It was a real honor to serve on this board for over forty years and as president for the past twenty-five years. In that forty-year span, this foundation provided over seven hundred grants to individuals and agencies interested in improving services to youth with disabilities in Minnesota. As president, I was provided a monthly stipend to manage the resources of this organization, another income source. There is a lesson to be learned from my work experience that hopefully will make sense to you. Participation in community activities has been a key factor in advancing my professional work career and financial status. Remember, it's more exciting to be a leader than a follower; leaders effect change more than followers. Leaders make more money than followers, and more money means a more enjoyable lifestyle and a more comfortable future retirement. So, just another reminder to get involved!

Overcoming Obstacles
Job obstacles will always occur; be persevering.

Jim Griffin, a good friend and officiating partner of mine, was one of Saint Paul's first black policemen. He worked as a train porter in his early work career, and after serving in the armed forces returned home and, with the aid of "veterans preference," joined the police force. Jim soon set his sights on being the first black sergeant on the force. He studied diligently, scored tops on the test, and became Sergeant Griffin. A few years later, his goal was to advance to the lieutenant position. Again, after taking numerous classes and considerable study, he was appointed Saint Paul's first black police lieutenant. When a vacancy for the position of assistant chief occurred, Jim rolled up his sleeves and set his sights on attaining this top-level position. To the surprise of many, he scored number one on this test and became the logical choice for this position. Historically the top-scoring applicant was always given the appointment. In this instance, however, the number two applicant was appointed to the job. Jim was in shock and figured the color of his skin was the reason he was being overlooked. I recall him saying, "If I have to mortgage my home and sell everything I own, I'm going to get that job. I deserve it!" He proceeded to hire one of Saint Paul's top lawyers, and his case was put on the court docket. An interesting outcome took place. The case was settled out of court in a unique manner. The police administration decided to appoint not one but two assistant chiefs, Jim Griffin being one of the two appointments. An interesting sideline occurred. The high-priced lawyer never billed Jim for his services, and after two years, Jim met with the lawyer and asked why he never received a bill. The lawyer said, "Jim, you deserved to be appointed to that assistant chief position, so I'm not going to bill you, but you tell everyone you know that I charged you plenty." Jim was unwilling to just give up and walk away without a fight. He figured he knew why he didn't receive that appointment and decided to take on the police administration and stand up for what he believed. You see, "giving up" was never in Jim's vocabulary! When you're convinced you are being treated unfairly on the job, you have a decision to make: take action, or walk away. Know your facts before making that decision. Jim felt he knew the facts; he acted and won, and it didn't cost him a nickel!

On the other hand, let me share a personal experience where it appeared I was being treated unfairly but, knowing the facts, decided to just walk away. In my midfifties I learned that the assistant commissioner for vocational rehabilitation position was vacant. I felt qualified for this job and decided to apply. This was a political position with great pay and benefits but offered questionable security. The job interview seemed to go well, and a few days later I received a call from the commissioner himself. He informed me that I was his number one selection; however, the governor felt affirmative action was more important, so the decision was made to appoint a woman for the job. I was disappointed seeing this large salary upgrade go right down the drain. I later learned that this woman appointed to the job lasted just one year. I thought, *Wow, if I had been selected for this job and suffered the same fate, I would be sitting on the sidelines looking for a new job at the State Employment Office.* Who knows, from a positive viewpoint, I might have been the greatest assistant commissioner the department ever had, but I'll never find out. That did it for me; at fifty years of age I made the decision to stick with my current job for the remainder of my work career. Being a conservative junkie, I was happy to have my current job and a pension and fringe benefit package that I couldn't afford to lose. Knowing the facts, maybe the governor did me a favor. Anyway, I was supportive of affirmative action!

Some obstacles seem almost impossible to overcome, but don't be so sure. Dan Fitzpatrick was a promising athlete just starting to make his way in life after graduating from high school. On a vacation trip one evening in the middle of Iowa, he made the fatal mistake of falling asleep at the wheel, which resulted in a catastrophic accident. When he woke up in the hospital he discovered he had no feeling from the neck down; his spinal cord had been severed, and he was labeled "quadriplegic." A few months later, I was assigned to be his rehabilitation counselor. Dan's adjustment to this catastrophic disability was very difficult. In the eight years following the accident, he had little interest in anything beyond that of survival. Then one day I received a call that he wanted to see me. He said, "I've decided that even though I've got this problem, I want to do something positive with my life. Will you help me?" Dan, through therapy and some adaptive aids, had gained some use of his hands. He was a bright young man with a great personality and now seemed highly motivated. Our rehabilitation agency provided him with some accounting training and an electric wheelchair to get around on his own. He was on his way! We later purchased Dan a van that he was determined to drive using adaptive aids; he did drive, believe it or not. In the years that followed, he secured employment with the local school system, bought a house that was adapted to his needs, got married to a wonderful young lady, and became an active member of the community. His goal in life was to coach, so it was no surprise when he ended up coaching the adaptive floor hockey team for one of Saint Paul's special education programs. Perhaps Dan's greatest contribution to the community was his motivating influence for other folks with disabilities. Dan had challenged himself to achieve as normal a life in the community as possible, even though faced with this severe disability. Dan typifies the best example of what can be accomplished if you refuse to give up and take the easy way out, doing nothing. Dan faced his future by "thinking out of the box" every day of his life to achieve goals that most of us would believe impossible. Those folks who survived in those challenging Depression times saw the bottle as half full rather than half empty. Dan saw the bottle as plum full! Your challenge is not to succumb to adversity but instead attack it head-on and, like Dan, fill that bottle right to the top!

All of us who survive in this life will be faced with problems that at times may seem insurmountable. The secret is to view these problems as challenges, as opportunities. My old boss had a saying that "problems are opportunities dressed in work clothes." His point was that problems are difficult to resolve while opportunities offer a positive and exciting challenge. The secret of a good architect, when faced with a difficult building issue, is to arrive at a solution converting this "problem" into a featured "highlight." In the home or building being constructed, making the problem an asset! This is exactly the approach you should take when things don't go your way, when your ideas are rejected, when getting that perfect job seems so remote, or when advancement appears to elude you. Don't give up and take the easy way out; instead "think out of the box" for a solution and convert that problem into an asset—an opportunity! Who knows, that problem may end up being a source of additional cash in your savings account. Be an optimist; don't let that bottle go empty!

Adapt to Change
Change is inevitable; be willing to change with change.

My dad began his work career as a machinist helper at fourteen years of age back in 1914 and retired forty-three years later in the same field. Most of my older relatives seemed to follow pretty much this same pattern, sticking with one occupation of their choice. The working world has changed significantly in these past eighty-plus years. Keep in mind that employment documentation indicates that most workers in current times might well expect to experience up to four different occupations in their working career. For example, my son served as a fueler on an aircraft carrier in the US Navy. After discharge, this experience helped him secure a job fueling airplanes at the Minneapolis Airport. This looked like a lifelong job until his company went on strike seeking a wage increase. The strike was unsuccessful, and he, along with other workers, was discharged. Over the next thirty years he progressively changed occupations from being employed as a truck driver, to a landscaper, a cement mason, and finally as crewman on a boat that serviced oil rigs in Alaska, and there is no guarantee more changes won't occur in the future. My son well exceeded that four occupations prediction. He is motivated to work and, as a result, willing to modify his employment as needed to meet current demands. I would describe his work career as being resilient.

My son's need to be resilient with a willingness to change occupations represents a major trend occurring in the current labor market. The introduction of automation, the use of robotics, and other job efficiencies are changing and reducing the number of unskilled and semiskilled jobs in industry. The outsourcing of jobs to other countries where labor is so cheap is another factor in the reduction of these laboring jobs. This dramatic change in industry leaves the unskilled or semiskilled labor force two alternatives: (1) consider some form of technical/vocational training or (2) be flexible with a willingness to change occupations whenever necessary to meet local employment needs, as my son is doing. I want to reemphasize that the days of beginning and ending a career with the same employer or remaining in the same occupation for one's working life is slowly becoming a thing of the past. Few things seem to stay the same in this ever-changing world. Take music, for example, the music of the '40s that our band plays is popular with the older senior set but is of little interest to younger folks. As we seniors die off, so will this music die off to be replaced by music of the current times: rock and roll, rap, and who knows what the future holds. Job security and job stability are also becoming terms of the past. Change is in every facet of our lives, so you had better be resilient, ready to adapt to change. I suggest you view these employment changes in your life not as problems but as opportunities. So if you are handed that pink slip for one reason or other, don't attempt suicide or turn to alcohol. Recognize that it is simply a part of our modern life. Adapt and move on!

A music friend attended Dunwoody Technical School in the mid 1950s to learn the printing trade. After graduating he secured a position with a large printing company in Minneapolis and appeared on his way to the security of a long-term printing career. After five years on this job, he learned that his company was going to relocate in Texas. He had no interest in leaving Minneapolis so decided to resign from this company. During this same period, the printing industry was undergoing a major transition into computer technology, and he discovered that the training he had received in the printing trade was totally outdated. As a result, he made the decision to change occupations. He said it was an emotionally challenging time for him but realized he had to pull himself up by the bootstraps and explore new careers. He changed occupations completely and began employment at a motorcycle shop both as a salesman and mechanic. After a few years, he made another major change and purchased half interest in a local bar/grill. This is another example of how advanced technology is dramatically changing many traditional occupations, requiring workers to be retrained or move on to other work. I remember my dad saying he could fix just about anything that would go wrong on a car, but when computer technology entered the scene, he was in deep trouble. He said, "When computer technology came on board, I was appointed job superintendent and no longer did actual mechanic work. My timing was perfect." He lucked out; no flexibility or retraining needed. What happened to my friend in the printing field is also occurring in many other trades, requiring workers to either be retrained or to move on to other occupations. Those workers unwilling to accept change are facing some interesting alternatives: to join the unemployment ranks or ask the spouse to be the family breadwinner. This may not be to the spouse's liking. Keep in mind that divorces are expensive, and your goal is to save money, not pay spousal support!

In my advanced age, I've come to the realization that most everyone's work careers will more than likely have their highs and lows—good times and bad times—but hopefully successes as well. It's simply the nature of the game of life. Whatever career you decide to follow, remember to always keep your eye focused on the future and not let those low periods and bad times lead you down a negative path. The success of your eventual retirement may well be hanging in the balance by the decisions you make. Simply put, think long and hard before you make a major job change that could put your retirement future in jeopardy. My dad's advice to me was pretty sound. "Never make a major life decision till you sleep on it." Maybe two or three nights of sleep is even better advice!

CHAPTER 9

Rule 3: Protecting Your Money

Maximize Your Savings
Use your money to make money; don't lose it.

Ridding yourself of debts and building that savings nest egg is key to maintaining an enjoyable lifestyle hopefully leading to a successful retirement. I've shared many different approaches and suggestions to eliminate or avoid debt and to expand your savings account. These suggestions were made purposely to stimulate ideas you might consider to maximizing your income level. Once you rid yourself of those nonproductive debts, and your income begins to grow, it is vitally important that you keep your savings in a safe place and hopefully use this money to earn additional savings. There are three fairly common approaches to saving money: (1) placing your savings into a bank or credit union, (2) investing in the stock or bond market on your own or with guidance from a licensed financial planner, or (3) placing your savings under the mattress for safe keeping, anticipating that your house won't burn down.

If your decision is to keep this savings in a bank or credit union savings account, be aware of the interest you will receive. This interest can vary dramatically depending on the economy and the bank itself. Check the interest rates at various banks and credit unions to be sure you are getting the best interest available; remember, interest rates can vary with each bank or credit union. If you decide to follow item two and personally invest your savings in one of various stock market plans or in bonds, it is absolutely essential that you seek advice from someone truly knowledgeable in investment practices.

The stock market can vary like the wind and is not a place for rank amateurs. If, on the other hand, you decide to utilize a licensed financial planner, take time to pick the right person that understands your needs. Visit at least three financial planners before you make a selection. Make sure the person you hand your hard-earned money to is licensed, has a positive track record, and understands your financial goals and concurs with your approach to investing, your risk factor (conservative or liberal.) Be aware of the fee structure and whether you will or will not be charged for each transaction the planner makes. In the 1990s, I decided to make a change from one financial planner to another. In making this change, I discovered that my original financial planner, in addition to his annual fee, had been charging an additional fee for each transaction he made. My new financial planner stated this would not be her practice, which resulted in a significant savings. This greenhorn learned a quick lesson!

Let me share another lesson learned the hard way. I had been very specific with my first financial planner that I wanted to follow an absolute conservative approach in my investment practices. I repeated this message many times. Being a conservative person, I wanted to take no chances of losing my investment. My adviser contacted me a while later suggesting an investment move that would guarantee positive financial results and was in the conservative range. I said to go ahead if this was a sure thing. A few months later this investment bombed, and I lost $5,000. He went directly against my recommendation to follow a conservative approach. It's important for you to select a financial planner who listens to you and can be trusted. Let me tell you it hurts right down to your toenails to see some of your hard-earned savings go right down the drain. By the way, if the stock market is your decision to follow, then be willing to hang in there with all its roller coaster ups and downs. The word is that those downs eventually rise back up, so they say! Now if "under the mattress" is your savings choice, realize that your cash will not earn a penny of interest. Also, as a precaution, be sure your home has sprinklers. Cash is very burnable!

I began investment practices in the 1990s fully understanding the need to deal with the ups and downs of the stock market and the importance of staying with the course. My second financial planner was right on target when her advice proved true, and the down market always seemed to recover in my favor. Today, in my late eighties, my thinking has changed. I'm not sure I have the time left to put up with those ups and downs, so I recently made the decision to exit the stock market and change to a financial plan that was more stable and offered a decent and consistent interest rate. This plan offers far more order and stability in my financial life. Younger folks have to understand that us old-timers worry more, enjoy a life of stability, and want a restful good night's sleep! We will let the young folks deal with the excitement and roller-coaster ride the stock market offers.

Legal Protection
Lawyers are necessary; amateur lawyers are not.

There is nothing I detest more than paying money to lawyers for services I feel capable of handling myself. I figured that a handshake, like in the good old days, was still the best way to do business. Well, folks, it isn't the good old days any longer, and forget the handshake. I learned the hard way that a lawyer ends up being your best friend when any legal or technical issues are involved. Save your handshake for greeting new friends. Let me share an interesting experience or two that helped me learn this lesson the hard way.

A close friend purchased a farm in northern Minnesota that had distinct fence boundaries defining his 120-acre land parcel. At the time of purchase the Realtor asked my friend if he wanted a lawyer to officially clarify the accuracy of the boundaries. My friend asked what I thought about this, and I advised him that hiring a lawyer seemed to be a waste of money. Well, two years later his neighbor claimed he owned twenty feet on the north side of my friend's property. The neighbor had hired a surveyor to survey his property, and this was the surveyor's findings. He claimed the original surveying, done some fifty years ago, was in error. This was a very upsetting situation requiring my friend to hire a lawyer to help resolve this matter in his favor. After two years of bickering and lawyers' fees, the case was settled in my friend's favor. Unfortunately, this legal haggling prevented my friend from moving full steam ahead with his farming operation. The thousands of dollars spent for lawyer fees, which was dedicated for the purchase of cattle, ended up in the lawyer's back pocket. I remember the lawyer saying, "Your friend may have won this case, but actually

I came out the winner, financially!" He was right, and if I had been smart and advised my friend to have a lawyer check the accuracy of the property lines before he purchased this farm, he wouldn't have wasted his money on lawyer fees. The initial cost to verify the property boundaries would have only been a few hundred dollars. I simply gave my friend bad advice! Although this friend won his case, he was forced to discontinue his cattle-raising operation because the legal fees had drained his farm budget. Chalk one up for my free advice! I think he's still my friend but, you know, I haven't heard from him in a year!

Let me share another example where I (Mr. Conservative) tried to save a buck by not hiring a lawyer and ended up with mustard on my face. I made the decision to sell ten acres that was part of my Cedar Hills property. To sell the parcel I had to allow entry to this property from my driveway, which was on the adjoining ten-acre parcel. We quickly had an interested buyer. At the property closing meeting there was unanimous agreement with the new buyer that entry to his property was to be at a specific location very close to the county road entry area. We both came to a handshake gentleman's agreement on this exact entry point. The real estate representative drew up the property sale document at his office and "out of the air" picked a random figure of 150 feet down my driveway from the county road entrance as the buyer's property entry point. I signed off on the document without a lawyer involved because both of us had agreed on this exact property entry location. They were going to build soon, and this entry point was agreed upon, so this 150-foot figure was of little concern to me. To make a long story short, the folks purchasing this land never did build their home and ten years later put this land up for sale. They told prospective buyers that entry to their ten acres was halfway down my driveway instead of abiding by our original agreement, using this 150-foot figure as gospel. By not having used a lawyer to legally clarify the exact location of this entry point I had, to put it bluntly, "screwed myself." You see, saving a buck doesn't always work out. I hope you get this message; you may not like lawyers, but they can save your "ash"!

So, without qualification, I'm telling you that lawyers are needed in our modern-day society as a sort of policeman to protect our hard-earned money. All lawyers aren't made from the same cloth, however, and it's important to hire one that is honest, that you can trust and that has your interest at heart. During my lifetime, there have been certain occasions when it was necessary for me to hire a lawyer. I knew few lawyers so checked with a few trusted friends and asked for their recommendations. I lucked out and used one of the lawyers that was highly recommended and his fees seemed reasonable; I liked his no-nonsense attitude and. his reputation was spotless. You should be aware that lawyers all operate using a different set of hourly fees. While serving as president of the Nevin Huested Foundation, I contracted with a lawyer from a large firm that charged a fee exceeding $200 an hour. I remember asking if his fees couldn't be reduced because our organization was a nonprofit foundation, and we had limited funds. To help us out, he referred us to a junior lawyer in his firm whose hourly rate was $180 an hour. So don't be bashful; clarify the hourly fee you will be charged so there will be no surprises. Be aware that a lawyer's pay clock starts when you are on the phone, meeting in his or her office, and when spending time on your case. It wouldn't hurt to plead poverty hoping they might lower their hourly fee for you; we conservatives never hesitate to cry a little "poor mouth"!

Like any occupational field, there are good lawyers, and lawyers that you should avoid hiring. This is why it's so important to get references from friends and to check out credentials. A neighbor of mine was a lawyer, who in his opinion, was tops in his field. This opinion was certainly not shared by others or by the legal profession. Apparently when money from a court settlement designated to a client's family ends up in the pocket of the lawyer, my neighbor, it's considered illegal practice. As a result, he ended up a disbarred lawyer but still a good neighbor. My point is simple; make every effort to employ a competent lawyer on all legal issues. Don't think you know it all and try and save a buck by acting as a "pretend' lawyer," as I foolishly did!

Trust Requires Proof
Signed contracts and references are safety valves.

Most of us older folks were raised to trust the folks we were doing business with, and a handshake closed the deal. Well, in the twenty-first century, I learned the world is different. I would again remind you to save your handshake for greeting friends because it simply is not an adequate means for closing any business transaction. Let me share an example of what I'm referring to. We wanted to build an attached porch on our country home. An advertisement in our local paper listed a contractor with thirty-plus years of experience in building home additions in addition to being bonded by the state of Minnesota. It sounded pretty good to us, so we met with the builder, agreed on a plan, and the price seemed reasonable. He talked a great game, so we gave him a $2,000 down payment to begin the project. I'm sorry to say our porch construction went on hold because we never saw or heard from this contractor again. After weeks of unanswered phone calls, we contacted the state Labor Department seeking whatever help they could offer, seeing he was bonded by the state. We were fed up with this contractor and wanted our $2,000 back. They suggested we take our problem to conciliation court for resolution of this matter and get our down payment returned. We followed this recommendation and months later were finally scheduled to present our case to the conciliation court in Minneapolis. The court decided in our favor, and as a result the state Labor Department returned our $2,000. They informed us that this @$#$% contractor could no longer do business in Minnesota until he returned this money to the state. What a hassle we had to go through to have this money returned. We not only had to go through this time-consuming court process, but it delayed our porch building project for nearly a year. It's good to be a trusting person, but when it comes to business matters, thoroughly check out the company you are planning to do business with. Get references regarding their previous work performance before you offer them a nickel; be smarter than me!

We ran into a similar problem when ordering carpeting from a small local company. We gave them a $1,000 down payment and discovered they had left town without delivering our carpet. We finally located them in Rochester, Minnesota, and they refused to return our money or provide the carpet. We again were forced to take the conciliation court route. We won handily, and they reluctantly were forced to return our $1,000. Now if I'm stupid and gullible enough to get ripped off a third time, I should be taken to court for stupidity! My point is a very simple one; when you work hard to build up a decent savings account, don't be willing to give it away by following poor business practices. I hope this point really sinks in. Learn from my mistakes. No, I'm not interested in buying that swamp land in Florida, and neither should you!

Avoid Sharing Your Savings
Being a "good guy" can easily reduce your savings.

You have a very good friend who has his eye on purchasing that new KIA Sorento. Unfortunately, his credit is marginal, and when he applied for a loan at the bank he was turned down. Over a beer he says, "I really need this car but the bank is so fussy. I earn a decent salary and can afford the car, but the bank has too many bureaucratic rules. If I have someone cosign with me, I can get the loan. Will you, as a friend, help me and cosign for this loan?" He really puts you on the spot; let's face it, it's hard to say no! Just remember, if you decide to be "good time Charlie" and say yes, you have just committed yourself to paying those loan payments if he fails to do so. You, as a cosigner, could be responsible for those loan payments on a car you will never drive. If you decide as a cosigner not to pay, your credit rating goes down the drain, so if you end up needing a loan, just forget it! Who knows, by being a good guy you may end up needing a cosigner yourself. I remember when working for the police department that a number of policemen would ask their squad car partner to be cosigners on loans. It was no problem for some, but I remember more than once it turned out to be a disaster. A lot of friendships went right down the tube when the "good guy" ended up being the "Stuckee." Cosigning for a loan can be dangerous and can end up depleting some of your hard-earned savings. For your information, my dad never cosigned for anybody, so I decided to follow my dad's lead. Now if your son or daughter needs your signature on a loan, that's a totally different scenario. Let's face it, loans to our children most likely end up as gifts; it's just worth it to hear your son or daughter say, "Thanks, Dad!"

Avoid Sure Deals
If the salesman's hair is slicked back in a ponytail, don't trust him.

Many years ago, my wife and I visited Puerto Vallarta, Mexico, looking forward to a one-week relaxed vacation in the sun. One sunny afternoon while walking on the beach, we came across this beautiful residential resort with a traditional Mexican architectural style. There was a sign indicating "available rentals" with the name of the resort, Los Tules. We were so impressed with the resort and beautiful setting, that we decided it would be fun to visit and see how the rich and famous live. We quickly learned that these were time-share rentals and frankly were surprised that a fully furnished one-bedroom rental right on the ocean for a two-week period was quite reasonably priced. This place was so impressive that we took the leap and decided to become time-share owners. Back in 1983, there was no high-pressure sales pitch for us to buy on the spot. The salesman told us to sleep on this deal before we made a decision. Our family has enjoyed vacationing at this resort for the past thirty years, and we have never regretted our initial time-share purchase decision.

The time-share business today, however, has radically changed since we purchased our unit in the 1980s. It you were to attend a time share-meeting in today's world, I would suggest you quickly enjoy the free breakfast, tell them you have another appointment, and run like hell. If you stay for the sales pitch, you will experience a series of fast-talking, never-ending, slick sales pitches and today's special, "Buy today; tomorrow is too late." There is simply no "go home and sleep on it" before you make a decision. The pressure is on to get your signature on the dotted line today, not tomorrow. If you fall for this pitch, it's your kiss of death. Remember, once you sign their contract, you are hooked. Their favorite techniques are to use three to four salesmen, one right after another, to talk you into their plan. If you turn down their first offer, there will be many much better offers to follow and numerous gimmicks to get your signature on the dotted line. These gimmicks might include a free airline ticket for next year's stay, a promise to freeze your maintenance fee at the current level, a guarantee you will actually make money by their unique rental plan, and if you decide not to attend the resort for a year, they will rent your unit and those rental funds are yours. It has been proven time and again that these are phony promises just to get your signature ... and your money. I could go on and on about the phony techniques used by these modern-day time-share salesmen. I know of what I speak! What began for us thirty plus years ago as a wonderful approach to vacation planning operated by honest and decent-minded businessmen is no longer true today. The current time-share salesmen cannot be trusted. It is a dog-eat-dog business with one goal in mind, to get your almighty dollar in their hands at all costs; lying and false promises are rampant! If you question my opinion, check your computer under the heading "Time-Share Problems." You will see I'm not alone in my opinion.

When you plan your next vacation, avoid all time-share salesmen. They are in every vacation location. No free breakfast is worth that four-hour pressure pitch. What will sound like the greatest vacation plan alive might turn into your life's greatest nightmare. Forget all about time-shares and look for good vacation deals in the paper or on the computer. It's no fun dealing with crooks who are really cleaver at stealing your hard-earned money; listen to the expert!

Double-Check Transactions
Don't ignore your financial statements; you could lose money.

Do you honestly believe that those detailed financial reports we receive monthly from our banks, credit card companies, and various retail stores are always 100 percent accurate? The answer is an emphatic no! These organizations are just as capable of making human errors as you or, perish the thought, your spouse. My wife, having been a bookkeeper, checks all financial reports we receive with the same intensity that a homicide detective checks out a crime scene. She also balances our checkbook each time she receives the bank's monthly report. It's not unusual to find mistakes hidden in these reports. It's kind of exciting to uncover those mistakes made in our favor but when in the bank's or credit card companies' favor, her blood pressure rises, and no time is wasted to seek an immediate explanation. There are so many ways to lose money in your various transactions with banks, credit card companies, or your local business accounts. Take the time to check these financial documents on a monthly basis. It's an absolutely terrible way to lose money by trusting the validity of all financial reports. Not long ago I made a bank deposit, put the receipt in my pocket, chatted with the teller for a minute, and when I arrived home gave the bank receipt to my wife. She noticed that the receipt showed one hundred dollars less than our deposit. She immediately contacted the bank and was pleased to learn they had already discovered and corrected the mistake; they even apologized! Don't forget that those folks collecting your money and imputing your data into the computer are human and can make errors just like you and me. Just this past year she uncovered at least four banking errors—three by the bank and one by us, I mean by *me*.

Avoid False Advertisements
Beautifully written advertisements and promises are not always true.

Many advertisements for products we see on TV and on Facebook are not always on the up-and-up. What you see and hear is not always what you get. Unfortunately, many of these products turn out to be substandard and of questionable quality. Returning the product to receive your money back usually ends up being a losing battle. Let me share another of my mistakes. I saw the advertisement for a book on TV that was of interest to me. I called the number on the screen to order this book selling for $19.50. The phone operator immediately described many other books and other products that I certainly would want. After fifteen minutes of saying no, she continued her pitch. Finally, in desperation, I told her to cancel my order, and only then did she shut up and reluctantly take my one-book order. I used my MasterCard, paying the $19.50 for the book in full. For the next three months, however, I was billed an additional $19.50 each month until my wife detected this overbilling. We contacted the company using their TV phone number, to find this number was no longer in use. Fortunately for us, the MasterCard company canceled this overbilling amount. This company was using a three-pronged attack to steal our money. First, the book was worthless; second, I received the hard sell to buy additional worthless products; and third, even though I paid the full price for the book, they planned to continue billing me each month for $19.50, maybe for the rest of my life. Here's an interesting sidelight to this story. A few months later, I saw on TV news that this book author was indicted and was heading to court. I wonder why? Heed my advice and don't fall for those phony ads. Everyone wants to tap into your savings account!

Let me share another example of white-collar crooks in action. There was an advertisement running on Facebook for a number of weeks describing a new miracle hearing aid for thirty-nine dollars. The claim was that this aid was of superior quality and truly revolutionary. The Facebook ad stated this product was equal to those more expensive aids that cost in the $2,000 range and were highly endorsed by a number of prominent people. I questioned this claim and decided to call the number on the TV screen and order the aid. The next day I checked my MasterCard report on the computer and was surprised to see that I was charged fifty-one dollars. I immediately called the company and was told the additional twelve dollars was for important materials that would come with the aid. I told her I didn't order these materials and didn't want them. Finally, after some discussion, she agreed to charge me just the $39.99. If I hadn't checked my MasterCard report, I would not have noticed this additional price update. The hearing aid arrived, and, as I suspected, it was worthless. It didn't fit into my ear and proved to be simply a cheap amplifier that sounded like it was in a tunnel. It was truly a scam that I'll bet profited this company thousands of dollars using false advertising. I checked the comments section of this Facebook ad and found that every comment was negative with findings similar to mine ... by the way, no returns and no money back. Don't be duped by these false ads that seem to appear regularly on my Facebook computer screen. If these phony companies have their way, they will drive you right to the front door of the poor house, with no money left to purchase that comfortable retirement rocking chair!

Savings and Gambling Don't Mix
The gambling table is the senior citizen's playground for losing money.

Fun at the gambling casino is spending twenty dollars on the slots, having lunch, listening to the music, and watching all the suckers losing their Friday paycheck or Social Security check. Gambling in excess of twenty dollars is dangerous and not recommended for amateurs; it's just that simple. If you become a gambling regular (I've avoiding using that word *addict*), you are putting your retirement planning in serious jeopardy. Don't be like my close college friend who, being a stubborn German, kept thinking the next blackjack deal was going to make him a big winner. One fateful evening he returned home to inform his wife he gambled his home away and would she please call their son to see if they could temporarily reside with them. That's a good way to lose your spouse. Be sure to check out all those gorgeous gambling facilities with all the trimmings. How do you think all those Indian residents earn their million-dollar-plus annual income? Don't kid yourself; they end up being the big winners not you! Ask that friend who just bragged about winning at the slots how much he or she spent to become the "big winner." Don't bother asking because they won't tell you the truth anyway!

Food for Thought

I'll say it once again; this book is all about making enough money to live and to retire comfortably. It's not about giving your money away. I suggest you read this chapter again. The way you decide to handle your money is vitally important. Place your hard-earned cash where it is safe and hopefully earns some interest. Don't be bashful about seeking help in regard to your financial planning. A lawyer can be your best friend on any legal issue. Deciding legal matters by pretending to be a legal expert yourself can end up being extremely expensive in the long run. Don't trust everything you hear or see, or that looks like a good deal. There are folks out there just waiting for you to earn lots of money so they can get their hands on it. Get a good night's sleep on any big issue that will involve your checkbook or savings account. Never spend more than twenty dollars at the gambling casino. Let all those big spenders lose their shirts. Check all your monthly financial reports from the bank, credit cards companies, and business transactions; they are not perfect. Take the time to protect your hard-earned money; let those millionaires give their money away. Again a reminder, rocking chairs aren't cheap!

CHAPTER 10

Thinking Outside the Box

Saying no is so easy; dream a little and say yes.

My older brother started his work career with a company called Engineering Research, located right in the heart of Saint Paul's Midway District. This company was focused on building something called a "computer" way back in the 1950s. In time, this company's name changed to Univac, later to Sperry Rand, and I don't know what it's called today. My brother was right on the ground floor in the growth of the computer movement. He graduated from the university in engineering and unlike me was a "thinker," always wanting to know how things worked, how an item could be improved, made smaller, run quieter, or go faster. One day he came up with an interesting idea to streamline an assembly line process that resulted in a major financial savings for the company. This led to a promotion within the company, to be followed by additional promotions, and in time he became CEO of his own computer-related company. He was a guy who was always "thinking out of the box." He was never satisfied with the status quo, always looking for a better way, or a new approach to solving a problem. This intrusiveness led him to a leadership position and a six-figure salary. He obviously inherited my dad's genes. I didn't! This became very clear to me in 1946, when I decided to enroll in the high school physics class. The instructor was calling roll when he came to my name and asked if I was Loren's brother. When I said yes, he expounded on how Loren had excelled in this class, had build a special suction machine they still used, and how he was a leading influence in his class. The implication being that I was blessed with these same talents. He soon learned that I ranked right at the top of his major disappointments of the year. My brother spent his entire career investigating and exploring new ideas, always looking for a better way! Who knows, with a little imagination plus a willingness to "think out of the box," you might find yourself in my brother's shoes ... and end up with a six-figure income. Don't be satisfied with "what is"; open your mind to "what can be"!

A good friend of mine loves baseball and wouldn't miss attending a Minnesota Twins baseball game. For years he was a longtime Twins spectator but now devotes part of his time at the ballpark aiding those fans who become ill, take an unexpected fall, or gets bonked by a foul ball off an errant bat. He is employed as a part-time medical assistant assigned to his favorite ballpark. In addition to his regular day job, he serves as a volunteer fireman in his home community, which provided the training needed for this medical assistant position. Just think, he gets paid for these duties, sees at least part of each game free of charge, and is doing something he loves. This friend represents a whole legion of folks who supplement their income with a part-time job to help make ends meet or to increase their savings account. He found this job because he was willing to "think out of the box" and came up with this unique idea to use his special skills in the baseball sports arena. His next goal is to pinch hit for the Twins, but unfortunately they won't issue him a uniform!

My daughter is employed as a nurse but has always enjoyed working with food, especially baking. Over the years she developed a skill in baking fancy cakes and decorating cupcakes. She has enjoyed making uniquely decorated cupcakes for various family and friends celebrations simply for her own enjoyment. This skill, however, has led to requests by individuals and organizations for her to provide specialized cupcakes at various events for pay. Her uniquely decorated cupcakes depicting various holidays or special events have gained considerable attention. She has taken on some paid jobs but is undecided if she wants to turn this hobby into a side business. She is aware that the demand is there. Now it's up to her to do some "thinking out of the box" as to the possibility and ways she might turn this hobby into a side business. By the way, her cupcakes are to die for!

Vern Schultz

In the late 1980s it was apparent that certain special education students that were eighteen and about to graduate from Saint Paul schools were not ready for independent living within the community. The staffers were unanimous in their opinion that these students were in need of additional, more intensive, life skills and job preparatory training before leaving school. A few of us came up with the idea of extending the school experience for these students until their twenty-first birthday. This was breaking with longtime tradition, so immediately most staff said it would be nice but couldn't be done. As supervisor I said, "Why not?" The responses were: "Well, it never was done before," "The state won't pay us foundation aid if they went through with the normal graduation," and "The district has no room for such classes," etc. My response was, "Quit thinking negative and why we can't do it, and, instead, come up with ideas as to how we can do it." In the course of some brainstorming someone said, "You know, it might even be better if we held these classes outside the school building because it would bring more reality into the picture." Another suggestion was made to not officially graduate these students at eighteen; let them walk across the stage but officially graduate them when they reach twenty-one. I suggested that if they didn't graduate at eighteen and their Individualized Education Plan required their need for extended education services, the state would be required to continue providing foundation aid. The result was that a new educational program was formed called "Transition Plus," which was housed in a non-Saint-Paul-school facility, with graduation occurring at twenty-one and the state continuing to pay foundation aid for these students. This program is still operating today by not only Saint Paul but by other school districts as well. This is an outstanding example of what "thinking out of the box" can accomplish.

Are you ready and willing to do some thinking out of the box? This book, so far, has touched on some varied ideas to secure supplemental income, to advance on the job, and to move up the employment ladder with the goal of putting more money in your pocket. I'm recommending that if you agree to "think out of the box" you just might identify a way to make money in a more imaginative way. Take time to sit back and think of those various ways that you perhaps haven't thought of yet that might identify a supplemental income source to your regular job. Another suggestion is to come up with suggestions that would improve your company's performance and save them money, leading to promotion potential and a salary boost. The key is to focus on the positive ways to achieve your goal and not on the negatives. Remember, it doesn't cost anything to think. Let me share a supplemental income source that I discovered that led to a significant increase in my savings account without ever punching a time clock.

The Stepping-Stone Plan
A way to make money for those willing to invest in sweat equity.

This supplemental income source arrived at my doorstep one day without ever realizing it was a moneymaker. I mean a good moneymaker! It didn't require a college education, a brilliant mind, a ton of experience, or a time clock to punch. If by chance this supplemental income source interests you, it will require a willingness to take a chance and to develop a bit of ingenuity along with a readiness to roll up your sleeves and get your hands dirty. You may even find it to be fun and satisfying. I did. Earlier in the book I suggested that you begin your early working life in a modest home, to avoid those upper-scale homes that are so appealing and loaded with amenities that might make your spouse happy but most likely strain or drain your family budget. Remember, a humble beginning in a starter home without all the fancy frills allows you to save some money and provides an opportunity to make money; that's right, make money by following the stepping-stone plan. If you follow this plan and are willing to use some of your personal elbow grease, I can almost guarantee you will make money. Here is how this stepping-stone plan works. First, when looking to purchase your home, locate the preferred neighborhood and check out those homes listed for sale that fits your price range. Second, check each home for defects in utilities (electrical, plumbing, heating, etc.), structural problems, water issues, and mold. Use a friend or acquaintance knowledgeable in home construction or employ a certified home inspector to assist you if needed. You most likely will want to stay away from purchasing a home with these types of major and costly problems. If the home is dirty or cluttered, if the decorating is out of date or in need of repair, or the outside curb appeal needs work, you have located the perfect home. It's exactly what you are looking for if the price is right. You want to purchase a home that is in a good solid state but in need of some updating. Correcting these problems is generally not too costly and can be carried out by you, the home owner. Many times, family and friends are willing to help you make these home improvements with the inducement of a few beers! Third, purchase the home by negotiating the lowest price possible. Make a list of the items needed to carry out this updating along with a suggested timeline for attacking each problem. If you are inexperienced in these home improvement activities, there are many "how to do it" books, home improvement workshops, and videos available either from the library or home improvement stores such as Home Depot, Lowes, Menards, Fleet Farm, etc. Guidance from family or friends experienced in home improvement tasks offers another excellent helping source. Fourth, attack each of your projects with enthusiasm and a willingness to put up with the mess. Each completed project will make your home more livable for your family and in the long term more salable. The home can be improved in appearance by work that you or your "helpers" can perform, such as tile, carpet, painting, roofing, redecorating, refinishing, etc. Identify work that will require limited hiring of those more expensive skilled tradesmen. The property's curb appeal with some elbow grease and landscaping efforts will also add considerably to the home's value. These added improvements should result in a significant profit well above the purchase price of this home when sold. This is money in the bank, and that's your purpose, to make money! Fifth, when your home improvement projects are completed, just sit back and enjoy the fruits of your labor. When time for another move appears appealing, and the Realtor's sale price of your home is showing a profit, then sell. Put your profits into the bank, or, if you are willing to use this approach for a second home to increase your savings account, implement this stepping-stone approach again. If you are up to it and motivated to earn additional money, then the sky is the limit as to the number of homes on which you might try this home rehabilitation approach. You decide when to quit. Some people love the challenge and go on and on while others quit after one or two moves. It all depends on your energy level, your partner's attitude, and how much money you want to make. By following this plan, your home improvement efforts will increase the value of your home, and when sold will earn you a profit. Believe me, this stepping-stone approach is a simple but smart way to make money and fatten your savings account.

The folks who make their living buying homes in need of repair and updating them for sale call their system "flipping houses," with no interest in living in the homes they purchase. Fixing up these houses is their full-time job not yours. You are not a house flipper. Your goal is far simpler, to purchase and live in a home while still maintaining a regular job, and to use your spare time and personal energy to upgrade this home for eventual sale and add to your bank account. Whether you use this extra income to immediately enhance your savings account or to help finance another home for similar upgrading that will add additional funds to your savings account is your decision. By the way, this home improvement work also has an added benefit. It's guaranteed to take inches off the waist line and make stepping on the bathroom scales much more enjoyable!

For years, I considered that going to the workplace each day along with some type of side job was really the only way to make a living. This stepping-stone approach, or making money away from the workplace, simply was not on my agenda. What's interesting, however, is that I found myself following this stepping-stone approach without realizing it. One day the lightbulb in my brain went on, and, to my amazement, I was doing just what this stepping-stone plan recommended, and it was paying off financially. Let me explain what happened. I purchased a starter home for $10,000 way back in 1952. This home was well built but had a leaky garage roof, no landscaping, an unfinished basement, and a small second-story unfinished bedroom area. I wanted to update this home to make it more livable, but, to be honest, I lacked any home building skills. I figured to learn on the job with some guidance from my dad, who could fix just about anything. After moving in, I rolled up my sleeves and proceeded to fix the leaky garage roof using tar I purchased from Montgomery Ward. It was a messy job that cost me a pair of shoes and tar-filled jeans that had to be thrown away. I also had to purchase turpentine to clean tar from my hands and face, but the leak disappeared, to my surprise! With the help of my dad we finished off the attic area for use as another bedroom, and I took on the project of painting all the walls in the living room and kitchen. We painted the basement walls a bright yellow that really brightened the room. The basement floor was discolored and dirty-looking, so we proceeded to paint it with a concrete-based paint and began to use this basement as a family recreation room. The yard was simply weeds and dirt, so I made about a dozen trips to the local landscaping company using my car trunk to haul the sod. I saved about one hundred bucks by hauling it myself. Did you know that with a little innovation you can also carry shrubs and even a small tree in your car trunk if you don't mind a filthy trunk? Believe me, the curb appeal to this home was improved by 100 percent. I was sweaty and dirty when I finished laying that last piece of sod, but the shower felt great, and that first rain made everything beautiful. It was my first experience in updating a home, and I found it to be kind of fun and certainly satisfying but dirty! With some assistance from my dad, I was gaining the confidence to try other more complex home improvement tasks. I loved it when my dad would say, "Is there anything I can do to help?" These were magic words to me!

Four years later we sold this home for $16,500 and used this tidy profit as the down payment on a new home we decided to have built in the West Saint Paul suburbs for $22,000, which was a ton of money in those days. The price of this home would have been considerably more if we decided to have the contractor give us a totally finished home. The home improvements we made in this first home paid off financially for us, so why not do some of the construction work in this new home as well and keep the mortgage payment down? I was up for it. Saving money was my goal! I had the fun of designing this home that saved us almost $1,000 and was excited to see the home move from blueprint to the completed project. With the confidence gained from doing some home improvement work in my first home, my wife and I rolled up our sleeves and decided to do all the decorating, varnishing, and painting, and saved more money by not building a garage, figuring that could come later. We purchased the sod from our neighbor's landscaping company and the shrubs and trees from an old high school chum who managed a garden center. Both gave us a discounted price. I saved a buck by laying each piece of sod myself and found I was fully capable of digging holes for the planting of the trees and shrubs. I must have a green thumb because everything grew beautifully with the help of a little rain and fertilizer. Because of the home improvement work we tackled, our mortgage payment was well within our budget even though the blue book value of this home appeared to well exceed my income level. A little personal elbow grease really paid off! I figured we would settle in this home for life!

After a few years, I realized that my perfect home design wasn't so perfect after all. I really missed the boat by not designing it with vaulted and beam ceilings that tend to give the home a more wide-open appearance. This vaulted ceiling concept with beam construction really appealed to me, so I began visiting open houses looking for this style home that would get my juices flowing. One Sunday afternoon we found the perfect house with a vaulted ceiling and huge beam construction in an upscale south suburban neighborhood. The home needed some decorating, landscaping work, carpeting, and cleanup work that we could readily handle. The asking price was $26,000, and we offered them a low-ball price of $20,000. To my dismay, they immediately accepted our offer with no negotiation; I should have been a little suspicious. The only negative feature we encountered was a plumbing lean that had not been taken care of. My lawyer indicated this was not a problem, and he would have it removed. We were excited about this move into another beautifully designed home, and put our home up for sale. It immediately sold for slightly over $30,000, another nice profit. Our home sale closed on a Friday morning, and that afternoon my parents babysat our children while we attended the closing of our new home. That plumbing lean was a worry to us, and when we learned at the closing table that this lean had not been corrected, I saw trouble with a capitol T. Plumbing problems can be expensive! Believe it or not, we considered this plumbing issue serious enough that we walked away from the closing table and canceled this home purchase. I was disappointed because I loved this home but realized we could have made a disastrous mistake with serious financial consequences. No wonder they were so willing to accept our low bid offer. When we returned home that afternoon and informed our folks what had happened, they went into shock wondering if we were crazy, and in absolute fear asked, "But where are you going to live? Remember you sold your home this morning!" I've learned over the years that parents worry way too much. It was true, however, that we had to find a place to live within the next few days. I viewed this unscheduled episode as a very significant learning experience: "Don't believe everything you're told, take time to check out the facts, and get a good night's sleep before you make a major decision." I remember saying, "But Dad and Mom, this home looked like such a good deal; sorry we put you in shock!" Well, life did go on as it always does. We banked our home sale profits and ended up renting a twin home just a few miles away. It was newly constructed with some work still to be completed, and the landscaping was pure mud. Our kids loved it! My parents fortunately avoided an ulcer and took a huge sigh of relief when they learned we located a place to live, and didn't ask to move in with them!

We saved money during the two years we lived in this rental twin home, so there was at least one benefit resulting from this unscheduled move. I still wanted that open style home with the vaulted ceiling and wood beams, so when the smoke settled, I sat down at the drawing table once again and began designing "the perfect home." You can bet it had a vaulted ceiling and huge wood beams! We purchased a lot on the side of a hill in South Saint Paul with an unbelievable panoramic view overlooking the Minnesota River Valley. We proceeded to hire a local contractor, and another home building process was begun. For me it was another exciting experience to see my home design blossom into reality. I'm not 100 percent sure if my wife, children, and parents shared this same excitement. Oh, yes, we did all the decorating, painting, and varnishing; decided not to finish off the lower level; and saved a couple thousand dollars by building a carport instead of a garage. I also did all the landscaping, which required my building a twenty-four-foot-long retaining wall that separated our home from the next-door neighbors' home. We kept the mortgage payment down by using our savings and doing so much of the grunt work. The house turned out just the way we expected with that striking vaulted ceiling with beams that gave us the wide-open feeling. I thought it was beautiful! Without question, we figured this would be our home for life. Sorry, not true!

Let me share another learning experience I wasn't prepared for. A good friend with a college degree in electrical engineering agreed to wire this home at a very reduced cost. I figured this was an outstanding way to save a few thousand dollars. My friend completed the job to our full satisfaction, but the building inspector refused to sign off on his work. His objections to my friend's work made little sense. My dad, who was a member of the machinist union, clued me in on the problem. My electrician friend was not a member of the local electricians' union, and apparently the inspector was not going to approve this job till hell froze over ... or this guy joined the union. Fortunately, my dad, who had connections in the local machinist union, came to my rescue and said he would take care of it. The next day approval was received. Another lesson learned in what life is all about: know the right people! Thanks, again, Dad, for teaching me those life skills they failed to teach me at the university!

Years back while playing town baseball in southern Minnesota, I became enamored with the friendliness of small-town living away from the hustle and bustle of the big city. I had this latent dream of someday making this move to a small town in Minnesota and maybe even living on one of those beautiful southern Minnesota lakes. Well, who would have ever thought this might become a reality? After three years in our "dream home," we were shocked to learn that the state had approved the construction of a new highway (Lafayette Freeway) that would abut our backyard, take our view away, and add all that highway noise. We were in shock. Here was another roadblock to face! How could we possibly contend with this unexpected development? We were ready to pack our bags and face another unplanned move, but from a positive standpoint this presented a perfect opportunity to make that dream of living in a small-town community come true. Once we learned that construction of the Lafayette bridge was a sure deal, we ventured some twenty-plus miles south of the cities and learned there were two available lots right on Prior Lake. One of these lots was located on Martinson Island, connected to the mainland by a quaint bridge. This lot really caught our eye. It had beautiful beach potential and offered a perfect home site. The price was right at $8,000, and we decided to purchase it. The only negative feature of this move would be the twenty-seven-mile drive back and forth to work each day. Maybe I should buy a float plane!

I drew up what I thought was a perfect house plan for this lot and submitted it to a local contractor, who gave me a firm construction bid of $23,000. We were all set to put our current home up for sale when the contractor informed me he had erred in his bid and that constructing the home really would cost $25,000. This additional $2,000 figure exceeded our budget, so we decided to cancel purchasing this lake lot and stay put. Six months later, the Lafayette highway construction was in motion, so we decided to bite the bullet and move no matter the cost. To our dismay we were informed that our dream lot on Prior Lake had risen in price from $8,000 to $18,000. Apparently, somebody either discovered gold on this lot, or the owner realized the lot's true value and decided not to give it away. At any event, we goofed by letting that extra $2,000 bid increase scare us off—another example of my ultraconservative upbringing! This $18,000 price was totally out of our price range, but our luck changed when we discovered a lot right across the street for $6,000 well within our budget. We purchased this lot right on the spot before it also skyrocketed in price. We also learned in that six-month period that the contractor's home bid had risen to $27,000. Darn that inflation! Our South Saint Paul "freeway" home sold quickly for another handsome profit, and our dream to reside in a small-town community and to live on a beautiful lake was to be a reality. We were slowly climbing up the ladder!

This move to small-town rural living really opened my eyes to the fact that each home purchase or building project we had undertaken thus far had resulted in a selling price that, without exception, exceeded the purchase price. It was obvious that our decision to roll up our sleeves and become directly involved in the building and updating process of these homes led to three outcomes: (1) I enjoyed involving myself in these home improvement projects and was learning home construction skills and was having fun; (2) each move resulted in a more expensive and updated home with more amenities, which would have normally exceeded my income level; and (3) the lightbulb in my mind suddenly flipped on. I was following that stepping-stone plan without realizing it. I had discovered an additional way of making money for my future retirement and was having fun doing it. I figured my approach to home building fit under the "thinking out of the box" category of making money without punching a time clock!

I wanted our new lake home to be built as reasonably priced as possible with a low mortgage rate. To achieve this goal, we worked out an agreement with the contractor that we would again do all the decorating, painting, wallpapering, beach work, and landscaping. By the way, I noticed that the sod was getting heavier with each move. A few years later when money permitted, I also participated in finished off this home's lower level to include an office, a recreation room with fireplace, a bedroom, and barroom. It was a lot of work, but in the process I gained considerable knowledge and experience in the techniques of home building. We lived in this Prior Lake home for eighteen years and truly enjoyed the fun and enjoyment of lake living. After our children left home in the mid-1980s, and lake living had lost a bit of its glamour, we again began to get that disease called "wanderlust." Maybe we just like the excitement of moving!

A few years earlier, my son had built a beautiful log home in the country with stately oak and evergreen trees in an atmosphere of peace and quiet. It got us thinking that maybe this type of relaxed country living would be the perfect setting to spend our remaining years. We had never experienced true country living with acreage, a pole barn, and, who knows, maybe a horse or two. If this was to be my final home, wouldn't it be exciting to design this home, be my own contractor, and actively participate in the home construction from ground up … do it all! I had accumulated three months of vacation time, already had designed my past two homes, and had gained valuable experience in various home construction activities, so why not take this giant step? I profited from each of my previous building experiences, so why shouldn't I make a bundle of cash in this building adventure as well? I was going way out on the limb never having had contractor experience, but it was a challenge I was willing to face. Apparently somewhere along the way I was abandoning my conservative approach to life. Sorry, Dad!

Up to this point of our life together, we had lived in the heart of the big city, in the suburbs, and in a lake setting bordering a rural community. This move would be to rural farm country away from stores, restaurants, churches, and next-door neighbors. We contacted a Realtor friend who specialized in the sale of farmland.

We asked him to find a ten-acre parcel away from town with land suitable for home construction that offered a panoramic view of the country. A week later, the Realtor showed us an eighty-acre farm that had recently been divided into eight ten-acre building parcels. He said this land was slated for sale that coming Sunday and would most likely be grabbed up quickly. One of these parcels appeared perfect for the home I had in mind. The building site was on a knoll with beautiful oak trees and a view in the distance of Fish Lake. I grabbed it immediately and on the spot made the decision to purchase the ten-acre parcel to the west of this property. Later, with approval of my wife, we purchased the ten-acre parcel to the east of this property. We had suddenly become land barons, and I loved it!

The acreage with the building site was purchased for $32,000, and each of the other ten-acre parcels sold for $28,000, for a total of $88,000. Now that I committed to this purchase, I had to figure out where I would dig up this money. That was no small challenge! I had no available money stashed away so agreed to purchase this land on a contract for deed: $600 a month interest and $1 on principal. I knew that coming up with this payment each month was going to drain me dry or send me to the poor house. Our solution was to immediately put our lake home up for sale. We took a sigh of relief when our home sold for a hefty profit of well over $200,000. I used this money to pay off the lots in full ... and suddenly became a rich land baron with money left over for home construction. At this point, life was good!

After selling our lake home, we temporarily moved into a brand-new rental apartment on Prior Lake. Darn it, they wouldn't allow us to do any updating. During the next two-year period, we had a driveway and pole barn constructed on the property. At this point my wife and I had reached a friendly stalemate regarding the house design. I desperately wanted to build a log home, and she didn't. At this point in my life I learned that life is just one compromise after another. We reached a compromise in an interesting way. While driving to Gig Harbor, Washington, to visit my daughter, I observed a home display by the side of the highway stating "Lindahl Homes," with a model of a beautiful country-style home that was quite impressive. The very next day I visited this company, which specialized in cedar-built, post-and-beam country style homes. The quality of the cedar they used was top drawer, and the post-and-beam construction was just what I was looking for. I took my wife for a second visit, and she enthusiastically agreed that this was the style of home she would love. Cedar siding was acceptable to her and to me as well. A compromise had been reached, not a divorce. The next spring the entire Lindahl building package was delivered in an eighteen-wheeler truck to our property, in March of 1989. My sons and I unloaded the contents from that truck to the pole barn on a slushy muddy Easter Sunday. We used a small tractor and hand-pulled a snowmobile trailer through the mud and slush to transfer these products from the truck to the barn. Believe me, my two sons would have much rather spent time looking for Easter eggs that day then playing in the mud, but unloading these materials ourselves saved us a bundle of cash! Remember, living through the Depression made me cheap. Sorry, I mean frugal!

Once the cement contractor had completed laying the basement block, it was time to roll up our sleeves and go to work. With the help of my two sons and a skilled unemployed cabinetmaker friend, we began the process of building this house. The cabinetmaker wanted to be paid in cash so was willing to work for a reduced wage, which was quite a savings for me. We contracted with the required tradesmen when needed, but the basic house was built to completion by the four of us. In addition to building the basic home structure, my sons did most of the electrical work, construction of the fireplaces, and all the tile work. A professional landscaper provided us with a basic landscape design, but the actual layout and construction work was done under the direction of my son who managed a landscaping business. Hundreds of field boulders from the site were used to construct a series of walls to enhance the beauty of the yard and to build a fish pond and waterfall. This home had many interesting qualities and was featured in the Minneapolis newspaper for its unique construction and total accessibility for the handicapped. It truly was our dream home and was built at a cost far below what a licensed contractor would have charged but was valued way above my income level. I must be honest, however, and say that if we had known the complexity of building this Lindahl-designed home, we may have taken another route; it was challenging!

I was beginning to truly enjoy this "sweat labor" approach to making money. It's a very simple premise: "The more work you put into a project yourself, the more money you will save." It doesn't take a Philadelphia lawyer to figure this out. I knew that eventually the money earned from the sale of this home would positively enhance my retirement income. By the way, I lost thirty pounds during this building project. In the years that followed, as money became available, I finished off the lower level into an apartment, built a covered patio, a year-round porch, a deck, and fenced in the entire thirty acres. At eighty-one years of age, we also added a mother-in-law apartment to our home but hired a contractor for this project. I still managed to do all the decorating, installed the insulation, and again did landscaping. Apparently participating in the building process was in my blood, or maybe I just enjoyed saving money.

Rental Income

My wife and I lived in this country home, called "Cedar Hills" for twenty-four wonderful years. In addition to the economic benefits, the personal enjoyment and satisfaction of accomplishing this building project were unbelievable. If I was forty years younger, there would be another of my dream homes on the drawing board, and it would absolutely include at least one rental unit and most likely two. This rental in the lower level plus the rental of the mother-in-law apartment resulted in $1,600 added income each month. It turned out to be an excellent supplemental income with very little extra work on my part, just a couple more waste containers to empty each week. These rentals not only resulted in another unplanned income source but added to the total value of my home when the time came to sell. Here was an extra income source that was like a gift. I really enjoy receiving surprise gifts!

We fully enjoyed this country living style for those wonderful twenty-four years. When I hit my eighty-fourth birthday, however, the home and yard upkeep was beginning to be more than I could handle, and the aches and pains of old age were beginning to take their toll. The thought of moving into one of those fancy retirement centers with all the amenities was beginning to look very inviting. We took the plunge in 2014 and put Cedar Hills, our home and acreage, up for sale. The home, including all thirty acres, sold for over $1 million, and we headed for the Kingsway Retirement Center and easy living. Who would have ever believed this "home improvement" plan of action, beginning with our simple $10,000 starter home, would lead us eventually to this million-dollar figure? If you enjoy getting dirty and sweating a bit, you just might try this stepping-stone approach, or maybe you have even a better idea to make some extra cash. Go for it!

CHAPTER 11

Seeking a Direction

My dad preached to us kids over the years that we should always try to secure a job with a government agency or with a large successful company. In both instances they would most likely offer an array of fringe benefits such as medical insurance, a pension plan, vacation time, etc. His opinion, based on living through the Depression, was that fringe benefits were more important than a big salary. In his mind, security was the number one issue in seeking work. It was his ongoing fear that another depression might be just around the corner. His influence must have prevailed with me because I followed his advice by spending nearly all of my forty-year work career in civil service government-related positions. I broke away from his influence just once when I took that daring chance and worked for the Sister Kenny Institute. As I indicated, taking that chance was my life's great gamble that proved to be no gamble at all. I realized that it was my conservative attitude toward life and work that was holding me back and discovered that working in a nongovernment setting also offered many advantages. Don't let your attitude hold you back. Now that I'm older and hopefully wiser, I'm not sure in today's world that my dad's conservative philosophy focused primarily on job security is 100 percent the way to go. I think his advice was right-on in those dire 1930s but not necessarily true in the changing world of today. Sorry, Dad, times have changed! I do concur however, that the Depression rule book (that mythical Art Schultz Economics 101 course) is just as valid in today's world as it was in those Depression years. It should be written in stone for all generations. If you agree to follow this rule book and rid yourself of unproductive debts, begin a savings plan early in your career, and are willing to take a chance and explore different approaches to expanding your income, I believe you are on the road to an enjoyable future retirement. Oh, yes, don't forget that word *sacrifice*!

It's been well over twenty-five years since the day I officially retired. I've had plenty of time to think back and contemplate my many life experiences—some good and some not so good. I'm in the twilight of my life sitting in this comfortable rocking chair hoping that you, the reader, in due time will inherit this chair and fully enjoy the fruits of your labor. This book was never meant to direct the reader into a special job or to influence a person's career direction. The primary purpose was to offer some suggestions on how best to perform on whatever job or career you select, plus some lifestyle guides leading to a successful retirement. It's purely in your hands as to the direction in life you decide to take. Having lived through that Great Depression, I've witnessed what it takes to survive some of life's greatest challenges. The challenges you face today are far different from those of the 1930s, but I believe the survival lessons practiced in those years are just as applicable in today's world. If living the good life and attaining an enjoyable retirement in the future is your goal, then I hope the suggestions offered by an old man pushing ninety years have given you some food for thought. Remember, from hard work and commitment comes increased income, an expanded bank account, an improved lifestyle, and a step closer to an enjoyable retirement. My rocking chair is just waiting for you!

Printed in the United States
By Bookmasters